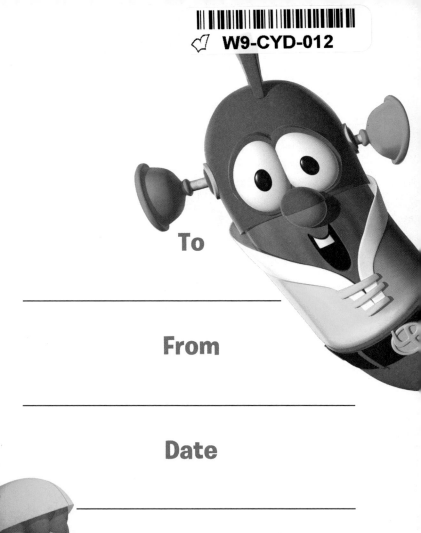

To

_____

From

_____

Date

_____

VeggieTales®

GOD MADE
ME
SPECIAL!

TM & © 2014 Big Idea Entertainment, LLC. All Rights Reserved.

ISBN 978-1-61795-381-1
ISBN 978-1-61795-363-7 (special edition)

Published by Worthy Kids, a division of Worthy Media, Inc.,
134 Franklin Road, Suite 200, Brentwood, Tennessee 37027.

Scripture quotations are taken from:

Scripture references marked KJV are from the Holy Bible, King James Version.

Scripture references marked NKJV are from the Holy Bible, New King James Version. Copyright © 1982 by Thomas Nelson, Inc. Used by permission.

Scripture references marked NIV are from the Holy Bible, New International Version®. Copyright © 1973, 1978, 1984, 2011 International Bible Society. Used by permission of Zondervan. All rights reserved.

Scripture references marked NLT are from the Holy Bible, New Living Translation. Copyright © 1996 Tyndale Charitable Trust. Used by permission of Tyndale House Publishers.

Scripture references marked NCV are from the New Century Version®. Copyright © 1987, 1988, 1991 by Word Publishing, a division of Thomas Nelson, Inc. All rights reserved. Used by permission.

Scripture references marked HCSB are from the Holman Christian Standard Bible™. Copyright © 1999, 2000, 2001 by Holman Bible Publishers. Used by permission.

Scripture references marked NASB are from the New American Standard Bible®. Copyright © 1960, 1962, 1963, 1968, 1971, 1972, 1973, 1975, 1977, 1995 by The Lockman Foundation. Used by permission.

Scripture references marked ESV are from the Holy Bible, English Standard Version. The Holy Bible, English Standard Version. Copyright © 2001 by Crossway Bibles, a division of Good News Publishers.

Scripture references marked TLB are from the Holy Bible, The Living Bible, Copyright © 1971 owned by assignment by Illinois Regional Bank N.A. (as trustee). Used by permission of Tyndale House Publishers, Inc., Wheaton, Illinois 60189. All rights reserved.

Scripture references marked MSG are from the Holy Bible, The Message - This edition issued by contractual arrangement with NavPress, a division of The Navigators, U.S.A. Originally published by NavPress in English as THE MESSAGE: The Bible in Contemporary Language copyright 2002-2003 by Eugene Peterson. All rights reserved.

Scripture references marked RSV are from the Holy Bible, Revised Standard Version. Copyright 1946, 1952, 1959, 1973 by the Division of Christian Education of the National Council of the Churches of Christ in the United States of America. All rights reserved. Used by permission.

Scripture references marked ICB are from the Holy Bible, International Children's Bible®, New Century Version®. Copyright © 1986, 1988, 1999 by Tommy Nelson™, a division of Thomas Nelson, Inc. All rights reserved. Used by permission.

Cover Design and Page Layout by Bart Dawson

Printed in United States of America

1 2 3 4 5—VPI—18 17 16 15 14

VeggieTales®

GOD MADE ME SPECIAL!

365 DAILY DEVOS FOR BOYS

WORTHY
Kids

a Message to Parents

I f you're already a fan of VeggieTales®, you know the importance of teaching your son the big ideas that are found in God's Holy Word. And this book of devotions can help you do just that.

This text (which is intended to be read by Christian parents to their young children) contains 365 brief chapters, one for each day of the year. Many chapters contain kid-friendly essays on topics such as honesty, kindness, generosity, and forgiveness. Other chapters contain Bible verses which can be discussed with—and perhaps memorized by—your child. Still other chapters contain easy-to-understand quotations from notable Christian thinkers. And every chapter contains a prayer.

During the coming year, try this experiment: read a chapter from this book every day. When you do, you'll have 365 different opportunities to share God's love and His wisdom with your son, and that's a good thing . . . a very good thing.

GOD IS WATCHING OVER YOU

For He looks to the ends of the earth and sees everything under the heavens.

Job 28:24 HCSB

Is it possible for you to figure out how much God loves you? Nope, God's love is simply too big for anybody to understand. But even if you can't understand God's love, you can still feel His love for you.

Today, remember that God watches over you, protects you, and cares for you. Be sure to give Him the thanks He deserves.

A VERY VEGGIE BRIGHT IDEA

He is the same yesterday, today, and forever, and His unchanging and unfailing love sustains me when nothing and no one else can.

Bill Bright

TODAY'S PRAYER

Dear Lord, thank You for watching over me. When I think about Your promises, Father, I know that I am protected, now and forever. Amen

DAY 2

THE RIGHT KIND OF ATTITUDE

Set your minds on what is above, not on what is on the earth.

Colossians 3:2 HCSB

God knows everything about you, including your attitude. And when your attitude is good, God is pleased . . . very pleased.

Are you interested in pleasing God? Are you interested in pleasing your parents? Your teachers? And your friends? If so, try to make your attitude the best it can be. When you try hard to have a good attitude, you'll make other people feel better–and you'll make yourself feel better, too.

A TIP TO START YOUR DAY

Remember that you can choose to have a good attitude or a not-so-good attitude. And it's a choice you make every day.

TODAY'S PRAYER

Dear Lord, I pray for an attitude that pleases You. Even when I'm angry, unhappy, tired, or upset, let me remember what it means to be a good person and a Christian. Amen

THE WORLD'S
MOST IMPORTANT BOOK

*But grow in the grace and knowledge of our Lord and
Savior Jesus Christ. To Him be the glory both now and
forever. Amen.*

2 Peter 3:18 NKJV

What book contains everything that God has to say
about His rules and His Son? The Bible, of course.
If you read the Bible every day, you'll soon learn
how God wants you to behave.

Since doing the right thing (and the smart thing) is important to God, it should be important to you, too. And
you'll learn what's right by reading the Bible.

The Bible is the most important book you'll ever own.
It's God's Holy Word. Read it every day, and follow its instructions. When you do, you'll be safe now and
forever.

TODAY'S PRAYER

Dear Lord, the Bible teaches me that it's
good to be able to control myself. So
every day of my life, I will slow myself
down and think before I do things. Amen

DAY 4

Obey Your Teachers and Listen to Them

And the world with its lust is passing away, but the one who does God's will remains forever.

1 John 2:17 HCSB

It's good to obey your teachers, but before you can obey them, you must make sure you understand what your teachers are saying. So, in order to be an obedient student, you must be a student who knows how to listen.

Once you decide to be a careful listener, you'll become a better learner, too. But if you're determined to talk to other kids while your teachers are teaching, you won't learn very much.

So do yourself a favor: when you go to school or church, listen and obey. You'll be glad you did . . . and your teachers will be glad, too.

TODAY'S PRAYER

Dear Lord, when I play by Your rules, You bless my life. But, when I disobey Your rules, I suffer the consequences. Help me obey You and my parents and teachers . . . starting right now! Amen

DAY 5

Always Be Honest

The honest person will live safely, but the one who is dishonest will be caught.

Proverbs 10:9 ICB

Nobody can tell the truth for you. You're the one who decides what you are going to say. You're the one who decides whether your words will be truthful . . . or not.

The word "integrity" means doing the right and honest thing. If you're going to be a person of integrity, it's up to you. If you want to live a life that is pleasing to God and to others, make integrity a habit. When you do, everybody wins, especially you!

A TIP TO START YOUR DAY

Unless you build your friendships on honesty, you're building on a slippery slope.

TODAY'S PRAYER

Dear Lord, help me to make decisions that are pleasing to You. Help me to be honest, patient, and kind. And help me to follow the teachings of Jesus, not just tomorrow, but every day. Amen

DAY 6

Knowing Right from Wrong

Lead a tranquil and quiet life in all godliness and dignity.

1 Timothy 2:2 HCSB

If you're old enough to know right from wrong, then you're old enough to do something about it. In other words, you should always try to do the right thing, and you should also do your very best not to do the wrong thing.

The more self-control you have, the easier it is to do the right thing. Why? Because, when you learn to think first and do things next, you avoid lots of silly mistakes. So here's great advice: first, slow down long enough to figure out the right thing to do—and then do it. You'll make yourself happy, and you'll make lots of other people happy, too.

A TIP TO START YOUR DAY

Good behavior leads to a happy life. And bad behavior doesn't. Behave accordingly.

TODAY'S PRAYER

Dear Lord, there is a right way and a wrong way to live. Teach me the right way to live, Lord, this day and every day. Amen

DAY 7

Very Big Ideas About What to Do When Friends Misbehave

To start your day, take a few minutes to talk to your mom or dad about what these two quotations mean.

A friend is one who makes me do my best.
Oswald Chambers

God has a plan for your friendships because He knows your friends help determine the quality and direction of your life.
Charles Stanley

TODAY'S PRAYER

Dear Lord, thank You for my friends. Let me be a good friend to other people, and let me show them what it means to be a good Christian. Amen

DAY 8

God Loves You

But the love of the Lord remains forever with those who fear him. His salvation extends to the children's children of those who are faithful to his covenant, of those who obey his commandments!

Psalm 103:17-18 NLT

It's a fact: God loves you. And, His love doesn't come and go. He loves you all the time, not just some of the time.

How can you return God's love? By praising Him, by obeying Him, and by sharing the Good News of His Son.

Today, offer a prayer of thanks to your Father in heaven, and then do your best to honor Him with your good thoughts, kind words, and good deeds.

A VERY VEGGIE BRIGHT IDEA

Though our feelings come and go, God's love for us does not.

C. S. Lewis

TODAY'S PRAYER

Dear Lord, today and every day, I will praise You for Your amazing love. You care for me, Father, and I will honor You now and forever. Amen

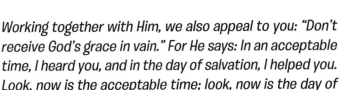

The Very Best Time to Forgive Somebody is Now

Working together with Him, we also appeal to you: "Don't receive God's grace in vain." For He says: In an acceptable time, I heard you, and in the day of salvation, I helped you. Look, now is the acceptable time; look, now is the day of salvation.

2 Corinthians 6:1-2 HCSB

When is the best time to forgive somebody? Well, as the old saying goes, there's no time like the present. So if you have somebody you need to forgive, why not forgive that person today?

Forgiving other people is one of the ways that we make ourselves feel better. So if you're still angry about something that somebody did, forgive that person right now. There is no better time.

TODAY'S PRAYER

Dear Lord, Your love is so wonderful that I can't really imagine it, but I can share it . . . and I will . . . this day and every day. Amen

DAY 10

GOD'S AMAZING LOVE

This is what real love is: It is not our love for God; it is God's love for us in sending his Son to be the way to take away our sins.

1 John 4:10 NCV

God's love for you is amazing. He's always watching you, always caring for you, always ready to hear your prayers, and always willing to forgive you, no matter what.

So, today and every day, give God the thanks He deserves. Praise Him for His Son, for His blessings, for His protection, and for His eternal love.

A VERY VEGGIE BRIGHT IDEA

Learn to trust God with a child-like dependence on Him as your loving, Heavenly Father. When you do, no trouble can destroy you.

Billy Graham

TODAY'S PRAYER

Dear Lord, I thank You for Your amazing love. You sent Your Son to this earth so that I can have eternal life. I will praise You now and forever, Father, for Your incredible gifts and for Your eternal love. Amen

DAY 11

Think about the Other Person

I pray that your love for each other will overflow more and more, and that you will keep on growing in your knowledge and understanding.

Philippians 1:9 NLT

There's an old saying that goes something like this: "Try to put yourself in the other person's shoes." It means that the more you understand somebody, the easier it is to forgive that person.

When you become angry with someone, try putting yourself in the other person's shoes. When you do, perhaps you'll be a little bit more understanding–and a little bit quicker to forgive.

A TIP TO START YOUR DAY

Kindness starts at home. So, it's important for you to be understanding of all your family members.

TODAY'S PRAYER

Dear Lord, help me be an understanding person, and help me be kind to everybody. Help me find people who really need my friendship, and help me be a good friend to them. Amen

DAY 12

AVOIDING PEOPLE WHO MAKE MISCHIEF

Therefore as you have received Christ Jesus the Lord, walk in Him.

Colossians 2:6 HCSB

Face facts: not everybody you know is well behaved. Your first job is to recognize bad behavior when you see it . . . and your second job is to make sure that you don't join in!

The moment that you decide to avoid mischief whenever you see it is the moment that you'll make yourself happy, your parents happy, and God happy. And you'll stay out of trouble. And you'll be glad you did!

A VERY VEGGIE BRIGHT IDEA

Christians are the citizens of heaven, and while we are on earth, we ought to behave like heaven's citizens.

Warren Wiersbe

TODAY'S PRAYER

Dear Lord, I still have so much to learn. Every day, let me learn from my parents, from my teachers, and from the Bible. And then, let me use the things I learn to make Your world a better place. Amen

GOD'S WISDOM CAN HELP YOU MAKE GOOD CHOICES

If you need wisdom–if you want to know what God wants you to do–ask him, and he will gladly tell you. He will not resent your asking.

James 1:5 NLT

Solomon wasn't just a king. He was also a very wise man and a very good writer. He even wrote several books in the Bible! So when He finally put down His pen, what was this wise man's final advice? It's simple: Solomon said, "Honor God and obey His commandments."

The next time you have an important choice to make, ask yourself this: "Am I honoring God and obeying Him? And am I doing what God wants me to do?" If you can answer those questions with a great big "YES," then go ahead. But if you're uncertain if the choice you are about to make is the right one, slow down. Why? Because that's what Solomon says . . . and that's what God says, too!

TODAY'S PRAYER

Dear Lord, there are so many choices for me to make, and I want to choose wisely. So, I will read the Bible and follow Your teachings today, tomorrow, and forever. Amen

DAY 14

Friends Should Share

The righteous give without sparing.

Proverbs 21:26 NIV

How can you be a good friend? One way is by sharing. And here are some of the things you can share: smiles, kind words, pats on the back, your toys, school supplies, books, and, of course, your prayers.

Would you like to make your friends happy? And would you like to make yourself happy at the same time? Here's how: treat your friends like you want to be treated. That means obeying the Golden Rule, which, of course, means sharing. In fact, the more you share, the better friend you'll be.

TODAY'S PRAYER

Dear Lord, sometimes it's easy to think only of myself and not of others. Help me remember that I should treat other people in the same way that I would want to be treated if I were standing in their shoes. You have given me many blessings, Lord—let me share them now. Amen

DAY 15

Praise God for His Love

So through Jesus let us always offer to God our sacrifice of praise, coming from lips that speak his name.

Hebrews 13:15 NCV

Today, take time to praise God for His blessings and for His love. Your Heavenly Father sent His only begotten Son to this earth so that you can have a glorious life in heaven. That's an incredible gift that's meant for you. And, it's a priceless gift that deserves your eternal thanks.

God loves you. Thank Him for His love right now . . . and keep thanking Him throughout the day.

A VERY VEGGIE BRIGHT IDEA

God passionately yearns to be in a loving relationship with the people He created.

Bill Hybels

TODAY'S PRAYER

Dear Lord, I will praise You now and always for Your eternal love, for Your countless blessings, and for Your Son, my Lord and Savior. Amen

DAY 16

Your Family is a Gift

Love must be without hypocrisy. Detest evil; cling to what is good. Show family affection to one another with brotherly love. Outdo one another in showing honor.

Romans 12:9-10 HCSB

Your family is a wonderful, one-of-a-kind gift from God. And your family members love you very much—what a blessing it is to be loved!

Have you ever really stopped to think about how much you are loved? Your parents love you (of course) and so does everybody else in your family. But it doesn't stop there. You're also an important part of God's family . . . and He loves you more than you can imagine.

What should you do about all the love that comes your way? You should accept it; you should be thankful for it; and you should share it . . . starting now!

TODAY'S PRAYER

Dear Lord, You have given me a family that cares for me and loves me. Thank You. I will let my family know that I love them by the things that I say and do. You know that I love my family, Lord. Now it's my turn to show them! Amen

Be Kind To Everybody

Mockers can get a whole town agitated, but those who are wise will calm anger.

Proverbs 29:8 NLT

A re you the kind of boy who is kind to everybody? Hopefully so!

Tomorrow, and every day after that, make sure that you're a person who is known for the kind way that you treat everybody. That's how God wants you to behave.

And, if someone says something to you that isn't very nice, don't pay too much attention. Just forgive that person as quickly as you can, and try to move on . . . as quickly as you can.

A TIP TO START YOUR DAY

Be kind to everybody. Even when it's hard to be kind, it's worth it.

TODAY'S PRAYER

Dear Lord, sometimes people behave badly. When other people upset me, help me to calm myself down, and help me to forgive them as quickly as I can. Amen

DAY 18

Keep The Peace

Love must be without hypocrisy. Detest evil; cling to what is good. Show family affection to one another with brotherly love. Outdo one another in showing honor.

Romans 12:9-10 HCSB

Sometimes, it's easiest to become angry with the people we love the most. After all, we know that they'll still love us no matter how angry we become. But while it's easy to become angry at home, it's usually wrong.

The next time you're tempted to become angry with a brother, or a sister, or a parent, remember that these are the people who love you more than anybody else! Then, calm down. Because peace is always beautiful, especially when it's peace at your house.

TODAY'S PRAYER

Dear Lord, You have given me a family that cares for me and loves me. Thank You. Let me love everybody in my family, even when they're not perfect. And let me always be thankful that my family loves me even when I'm not perfect. Amen

DAY 19

TRY TO BE PATIENT

Knowledge begins with respect for the Lord, but fools hate wisdom and self-control.

Proverbs 1:7 NCV

The Bible tells us that we should be patient with everybody, not just with parents, teachers, and friends. In the eyes of God, all people are very important, so we should treat them that way.

Of course it's easy to be nice to the people we want to impress, but what about everybody else? Jesus gave us clear instructions: He said that when we do a good deed for someone less fortunate than we are, we have also done a good deed for our Savior. And as Christians, that's exactly what we are supposed to do!

A TIP TO START YOUR DAY

Speak respectfully to everybody, starting with parents, grandparents, teachers, and adults . . . but don't stop there. Be respectful of everybody, including yourself!

TODAY'S PRAYER

Dear Lord, please help me show respect for all people, starting with my family and my friends. Amen

DAY 20

Yes, Jesus Loves You!

You're blessed when you're content with just who you are—no more, no less. That's the moment you find yourselves proud owners of everything that can't be bought.

Matthew 5:5 MSG

Have you heard the song "Jesus Loves Me"? Probably so. It's a happy song that should remind you of this important fact: Jesus loves you very much.

When you invite Jesus into your heart, He'll protect you forever. If you have problems, He'll help you solve them. When you aren't perfect, He'll still love you. If you feel sorry or sad, He can help you feel better.

Yes, Jesus loves you . . . and you should love yourself. So the next time you feel sad about yourself . . . or something that you've done . . . remember that Jesus loves you, your family loves you, and you should feel that way, too.

A TIP TO START YOUR DAY

When God made you, He made a very special, one-of-a-kind person. So don't forget this fact: you're very special.

TODAY'S PRAYER

Dear Lord, when I give my heart to You, I become better and stronger. Thank You, Lord, for filling my heart with strength, with hope, and with love. Amen

DAY 21

ABOUT BARNABAS

Barnabas was a good man, full of the Holy Spirit and full of faith.

Acts 11:23-24 ICB

Barnabas was a leader in the early Christian church who was known for his kindness and for his ability to encourage others. Because of Barnabas, many people were introduced to Christ.

We become like Barnabas when we speak kind words to our families and to our friends. And then, because we have been generous and kind, the people around us can see how Christians should behave. So when in doubt, be kind and generous to others, just like Barnabas.

A TIP TO START YOUR DAY

Be an encourager! Barnabas was known as a man who encouraged others. He made other people feel better by saying kind things. You, like Barnabas, can encourage your family and friends . . . and you should.

TODAY'S PRAYER

Dear Lord, let me celebrate the victories of others. Teach me how to encourage other people. And let my words and actions be worthy of Your Son. Amen

Everybody Makes Mistakes, But Not Everybody Learns from Them

Instead, God has chosen the world's foolish things to shame the wise, and God has chosen the world's weak things to shame the strong.

1 Corinthians 1:27 HCSB

D o you make mistakes? Of course you do . . . everybody does. When you make a mistake, you must try your best to learn from it so that you won't make the very same mistake again. And, if you have hurt someone—or if you have disobeyed God—you must ask for forgiveness.

Remember: mistakes are a part of life, but the biggest mistake you can make is to keep making the same mistake over and over and over again.

TODAY'S PRAYER

Dear Lord, sometimes I make mistakes. When I do, forgive me, Father. And help me learn from my mistakes so that I can be a better person and a better example to my friends and family. Amen

Jesus Can Take Care of Our Problems

Do not love the world or the things that belong to the world. If anyone loves the world, love for the Father is not in him.

1 John 2:15 HCSB

An old hymn contains the words, "This world is not my home; I'm just passing through." Thank goodness! This crazy world can be a place of trouble and danger. Thankfully, your real home is heaven, a place where you can live forever with Jesus.

Jesus has overcome the troubles of this world. We should trust Him, and we should obey His commandments. When we do, we are forever blessed by the Son of God and His Father in heaven.

TODAY'S PRAYER

Dear Lord, I want to follow Your rules and follow Your Son. So, instead of trying to impress other people, I'll try to please You. Amen

DAY 24

TRY TO MEMORIZE THIS VERSE

*And remember, I am with you always,
to the end of the age.*

Matthew 28:20 HCSB

*These are words that Jesus spoke.
Practice saying this verse several times.
And then, talk to your mom or dad about
exactly what the verse means . . .*

A TIP FOR PARENTS
Today, talk to your child about . . . God's love.

TODAY'S PRAYER
Dear Lord, You have promised to protect me today and every day. I thank You, Father, for never leaving me, not even for a moment. Amen

DAY 25

Your Continual Feast

A cheerful heart has a continual feast.

Proverbs 15:15 HCSB

What is a continual feast? It's a little bit like a non-stop birthday party: fun, fun, and more fun! The Bible tells us that a cheerful heart can make life like a continual feast, and that's something worth working for.

Where does cheerfulness begin? It begins inside each of us; it begins in the heart. So please be thankful to God for His blessings, and let's show our thanks by sharing good cheer wherever we go. This old world needs all the cheering up it can get . . . and so do we!

A VERY VEGGIE BRIGHT IDEA

When we bring sunshine into the lives of others, we're warmed by it ourselves. When we spill a little happiness, it splashes on us.

Barbara Johnson

TODAY'S PRAYER

Dear Lord, I have so many blessings. Help me count those blessings and be glad. And, let Your love live in my heart this day and forever. Amen

DAY 26

Patience Pays

Be gentle to all, able to teach, patient.

2 Timothy 2:24 NKJV

The Bible tells us that it's good to be patient. But for most of us, it's also hard to be patient. After all, we have many things that we want, and we want them NOW! But the Bible tells us that we must learn to wait patiently for the things that God has in store for us.

Are you having trouble being patient? If so, remember that patience takes practice, and lots of it, so keep trying. And if you make a mistake, don't be too upset. After all, if you're going to be a really patient person, you shouldn't just be patient with others, you should also be patient with yourself.

TODAY'S PRAYER

Lord, sometimes it's very hard to be a patient person, and that's exactly when I should try my hardest to be patient. Help me to follow Your commandments by being a patient, loving Christian, even when it's hard. Amen

iF FRiENDS MiSBEHAVE, DON'T iMiTATE THEM

Stay away from a foolish man; you will gain no knowledge from his speech.

Proverbs 14:7 HCSB

If your friends misbehave, do you misbehave right along with them, or do you tell them to stop? Usually, it's much easier to go along with your friends, even if you know they're misbehaving. But it's always better to do the right thing, even if it's hard.

Sometimes, grown-ups must stand up for the things they believe in. When they do, it can be hard for them, too. But the Bible tells us over and over again that we should do the right thing, not the easy thing.

When your friends misbehave, it can spoil everything. So if your friends behave badly, don't copy them! And if your friends keep behaving badly, choose different friends.

TODAY'S PRAYER

Dear Lord, when other people misbehave, I know that I shouldn't join in. So help me do the right thing, Lord, even when others are doing the wrong thing. Amen

When You're Having a Hard Day

We take the good days from God—why not also the bad days?

Job 2:10 MSG

Face it: some days are better than others. But even on the days when you don't feel very good, God never leaves you for even a moment. So if you need assistance, you can always pray to God, knowing that He will listen and help.

If you're feeling unhappy, talk things over with God, and while you're at it, be sure and talk things over with your parents, too. And remember this: the sooner you start talking, the sooner things will get better.

TODAY'S PRAYER

Dear Lord, some days are easier than other days. When I'm having a hard day, I'll turn to You and say my prayers. And I'll talk to my parents. When I do, I know that things will get better soon. Amen

DAY 29

THE COURAGE TO TELL THE TRUTH

And you shall know the truth, and the truth shall make you free.

John 8:32 NKJV

Sometimes, we're afraid of what might happen if we tell the truth. And sometimes, instead of doing the courageous thing, we do the unwise thing: we lie.

When we're fearful, we can and should find strength from friends, from family members, and from God.

So if you're afraid to tell the truth, don't be! Keep looking until you find the courage to be honest. Then, you'll discover it's not the truth that you should be afraid of; it's those troublesome, pesky lies!

TODAY'S PRAYER

Dear Lord, sometimes it's hard to tell the truth. When I am fearful of telling the truth, give me the courage to do the right thing. Give me the courage to be truthful. Amen

DAY 30

is The GoLDen RuLe Your Rule?

Don't be selfish . . . . Be humble, thinking of others as better than yourself.

Philippians 2:3 TLB

Is the Golden Rule your rule, or is it just another Bible verse that goes in one ear and out the other? Jesus made Himself perfectly clear: He instructed you to treat other people in the same way that you want to be treated. But sometimes, especially when you're feeling pressure from friends, or when you're tired or upset, obeying the Golden Rule can seem like an impossible task–but it's not. So be kind to everybody and obey God's rule, the Golden Rule, that is.

A VERY VEGGIE BRIGHT IDEA

The Golden Rule starts at home, but it should never stop there.

Marie T. Freeman

TODAY'S PRAYER

Dear Lord, the Golden Rule is Your rule. And, I'll try hard to make it my rule, too. Amen

DAY 31

Honesty is a Habit

Those who want to do right more than anything else are happy. God will fully satisfy them.

Matthew 5:6 ICB

Our lives are made up of lots and lots of habits. And the habits we choose help determine the kind of people we become. If we choose habits that are good, we are happier and healthier. If we choose habits that are bad, then it's too bad for us!

Honesty, like so many other things, is a habit. And it's a habit that is right for you.

Do you want to grow up to become the kind of man that God intends for you to be? Then get into the habit of being honest with everybody. You'll be glad you did . . . and so will God!

TODAY'S PRAYER

Dear Lord, some habits are good, and some habits aren't. I know that it's good to be an honest person. So please help me form the habit of being honest with my parents, with my teachers, and my with friends. Amen

DAY 32

STARTING YOUR DAY WITH GOD

It is good to give thanks to the Lord, to sing praises to the Most High. It is good to proclaim your unfailing love in the morning, your faithfulness in the evening.

Psalm 92:1-2 NLT

How do you start your day? Do you sleep till the last possible moment and then hop out of bed without giving a single thought to God? Hopefully not. If you're smart, you'll start your day with a prayer of thanks to your Heavenly Father.

Each new day is a gift from God, and if you're wise, you'll spend a few quiet moments thanking the Giver. It's a wonderful way to start your day.

A TIP TO START YOUR DAY

Make an appointment with God every day, and keep it. Reading your Bible and saying your prayers are important things to do. Very important. So please don't forget to talk with God every day.

TODAY'S PRAYER

Dear Lord, the Bible teaches me that I should turn to You often, and that's what I will do every day of my life.

DAY 33

GOD'S PERFECT LOVE

We know how much God loves us, and we have put our trust in him. God is love, and all who live in love live in God, and God lives in them.

1 John 4:16 NLT

The Bible makes this promise: God is love. It's a big promise, a very important description of what God is and how God works. God's love is perfect. When we open our hearts to His love, we are blessed and we are protected.

Today, offer sincere prayers of thanksgiving to your Heavenly Father. He loves you now and throughout all eternity. Open your heart to His presence and His love.

A VERY VEGGIE BRIGHT IDEA

Love has its source in God, for love is the very essence of His being.

Kay Arthur

TODAY'S PRAYER

Dear Lord, the Bible teaches me that You are love. And, I know that You love me. I will accept Your love–and share it–now and always. Amen

DAY 34

Be Thankful!

Our prayers for you are always spilling over into thanksgivings. We can't quit thanking God our Father and Jesus our Messiah for you!

Colossians 1:3 MSG

A re you a thankful boy? You should be! Whether you realize it or not, you have much to be thankful for. And who has given you all the blessings you enjoy? Your parents are responsible, of course. But all of your blessings really start with God.

All of us should make thanksgiving a habit. Since we have been given so much, the least we can do is say "Thank You" to the One who has given us more blessings than we can possibly ever count.

A VERY VEGGIE BRIGHT IDEA

No duty is more important than that of returning thanks.

St. Ambrose

TODAY'S PRAYER

Lord, You have plans for my life that are better than I can imagine. I will trust You to take care of my future, and I will try my best to obey Your rules, now and always. Amen

DAY 35

Kindness Starts with You

Be kind to one another, tender-hearted, forgiving each other, just as God in Christ also has forgiven you.

Ephesians 4:32 NASB

If you're waiting for other people to be nice to you before you're nice to them, you've got it backwards. Kindness starts with you! You see, you can never control what other people will say or do, but you can control your own behavior.

The Bible tells us that we should never stop doing good deeds as long as we live. Kindness is God's way, and it should be our way, too.

A TIP TO START YOUR DAY

The best time to be kind is now, so get busy. Your family and friends need all the kindness they can get!

TODAY'S PRAYER

Dear Lord, sometimes it's easy to be nice to people and sometimes it's not so easy. When it's hard to be kind, Lord, help me say the right things and do the right things. Amen

DAY 36

He Cares for You

I will lift up my eyes to the hills–From whence comes my help? My help comes from the Lord, Who made heaven and earth.

Psalm 121:1-2 NKJV

God cares about you. His love for you is amazing; it's a love that doesn't depend on the way you behave. Even when you make mistakes, God still loves you.

God wants the very best for you today, tomorrow, and forever. So, thank Him for His love . . . today, tomorrow, and forever.

A VERY VEGGIE BRIGHT IDEA

Life in God is a great big hug that lasts forever!

Barbara Johnson

TODAY'S PRAYER

Dear Lord, thank You for caring about me. Because I am loved by You, I don't need to worry about things–I know You will protect me now and forever. Amen

How Would Jesus Behave?

And he saith unto them, follow me, and I will make you fishers of men. And they straightway left their nets, and followed him.

Matthew 4:19-20 KJV

If Jesus were here, how would He behave? He would be loving and forgiving. He would worship God with sincere devotion. He would serve other people, and He would always abide by the Golden Rule. If Jesus were here, He would stand up for truth and speak out against evil.

We read in the Bible that Jesus wants each of us to do our best to be like Him. We can't be perfect Christians, but we can do our best to obey God's commandments and to follow Christ's example. When we do so, we bring honor to the One who gave His life for each of us.

A TIP TO START YOUR DAY

When you have an important decision to make, stop for a minute and think about how Jesus would behave if He were in your shoes.

TODAY'S PRAYER

Heavenly Father, I give thanks for my church and for the opportunity to worship there. Amen

DAY 38

iT's imporTanT To make Time For God

I wait quietly before God, for my hope is in him.

Psalm 62:5 NLT

When it comes to spending time with God, are you a "squeezer" or a "pleaser"? Do you squeeze God into your schedule with a prayer before mealtime, or do you please God by talking to Him far more often than that? If you're wise, you'll form the habit of spending time with God every day.

Even if you're the busiest boy on Planet Earth, you can still carve out a little time for God. And when you think about it, isn't that the very least you should do?

A TIP TO START YOUR DAY

The world is constantly vying for your attention, and sometimes the noise can be deafening. Remember the words of Elisabeth Elliot; she said, "The world is full of noise. Let us learn the art of silence, stillness, and solitude."

TODAY'S PRAYER

Lord, let me worship You every day of my life, and let me discover the peace that can be mine when I welcome You into my heart. Amen

DAY 39

You Can Return God's Love by Obeying His Commandments

But be doers of the word and not hearers only.

James 1:22 HCSB

How can you show God how much you love Him? By obeying His commandments, that's how! When you follow God's rules, you show Him that you have real respect for Him and for His Son.

Sometimes, you will be tempted to disobey God, but don't do it. And sometimes you'll be tempted to disobey your parents or your teachers . . . but don't do that, either.

When your parent steps away or a teacher looks away, it's up to you to control yourself. And of this you can be sure: if you really want to control yourself, you can do it!

A TIP TO START YOUR DAY

Make friends with people who, by their words and actions, encourage you to obey God.

TODAY'S PRAYER

Dear Lord, I want to be an obedient person. Help me understand Your rules and obey them. Amen

DAY 40

iT's a GreaT Day
To CeLebraTe LiFe!

Celebrate God all day, every day. I mean, revel in him!

Philippians 4:4 MSG

What kind of day are you expecting to have? Are you determined to celebrate the life God has given you? Hopefully so! Are you expecting God to do wonderful things? Hopefully so! Are you happy about your family, your friends, and your church? Hopefully so! After all, God loves you, and that fact should make you very happy indeed. So treat this day as a big celebration . . . because that's exactly what it should be.

A TIP TO START YOUR DAY

God has given you the gift of life (here on earth) and the promise of eternal life (in heaven). Now, He wants you to celebrate those gifts.

TODAY'S PRAYER

Dear Lord, today I will try my best to keep joy in my heart. I will celebrate the life You have given me here on earth and the eternal life that will be mine in heaven. Amen

DAY 41

Very Big ideas about Self-Control

To start your day, take a few minutes to talk to your mom or dad about what these two quotations mean.

Your thoughts are the determining factor as to whose mold you are conformed to. Control your thoughts and you control the direction of your life.

Charles Stanley

If you'd like more self-control, ask God to help you slow down and think before you act.

Criswell Freeman

TODAY'S PRAYER

Dear Lord, I want to be able to control myself better and better each day. Help me find better ways to behave myself in ways that are pleasing to You. Amen

DAY 42

THINK BEFORE YOU SPEAK

To everything there is a season . . . a time to keep silence, and a time to speak.

Ecclesiastes 3:1, 7 KJV

Sometimes, it's easier to say the wrong thing than it is to say the right thing—especially if we're in a hurry to blurt out the first words that come into our heads. But, if we are patient and if we choose our words carefully, we can help other people feel better, and that's exactly what God wants us to do.

The Book of Proverbs tells us that the right words, spoken at the right time, can be wonderful gifts to our families and to our friends. That's why we should think about the things that we say before we say them, not after. When we do, our words make the world a better place, and that's exactly what God wants!

TODAY'S PRAYER

Dear Lord, when I'm about to say something, help me think about my words before I say them, not after. Amen

DAY 43

Jesus Loves You!

Just as the Father has loved Me, I also have loved you. Remain in My love.

John 15:9 HCSB

The Bible makes this promise: Jesus loves you. And how should that make you feel? Well, the fact that Jesus loves you should make you very happy indeed, so happy, in fact, that you try your best to do the things that Jesus wants you to do.

Jesus wants you to welcome Him into your heart, He wants you to love and obey God, and He wants you to be kind to people. These are all very good things to do . . . and the rest is up to you!

A TIP TO START YOUR DAY

Jesus loves you so much that He gave His life so that you might live forever with Him. And how can you repay Christ's love? By accepting Him into your heart and by obeying His rules. When you do, He will love you and bless you forever.

TODAY'S PRAYER

Dear Jesus, I thank You for Your love, a love that never ends. I will return Your love and I will share it with the world. Amen

DAY 44

CHOOSING WISELY

I am offering you life or death, blessings or curses. Now, choose life! . . . To choose life is to love the Lord your God, obey him, and stay close to him.

Deuteronomy 30:19-20 NCV

Choices, choices, choices! You've got so many choices to make, and sometimes, making those choices isn't easy. At times you're torn between what you want to do and what you ought to do. When that happens, it's up to you to choose wisely . . . or else!

When you make wise choices, you are rewarded; when you make unwise choices, you must accept the consequences. It's as simple as that. So make sure that your choices are pleasing to God . . . or else!

TODAY'S PRAYER

Dear God, I have many choices to make. Help me choose wisely as I follow in the footsteps of Your Son, Jesus. Amen

DAY 45

YOUR ATTITUDE

Make your own attitude that of Christ Jesus.

Philippians 2:5 HCSB

What's an attitude? The word "attitude" means "the way that you think." And don't forget this: your attitude is important.

Your attitude can make you happy or sad, grumpy or glad, joyful or mad. And, your attitude doesn't just control the way that you think; it also controls how you behave. If you have a good attitude, you'll behave well. And if you have a bad attitude, you're more likely to misbehave.

Have you spent any time thinking about the way that you think? Do you pay much attention to your attitude? Hopefully so! After all, a good attitude is better than a bad one . . . lots better.

You have more control over your attitude than you think. So do your best to make your attitude a good attitude. One way you can do that is by learning about Jesus and about His attitude toward life. When you do, you'll learn that it's always better to think good thoughts, and it's always better to do good things. Always!

TODAY'S PRAYER

Dear Lord, help me have an attitude that is pleasing to You. And, let me remember to count my blessings today, tomorrow, and every day after that. Amen

DAY 46

TRY TO MEMORIZE THIS VERSE

*For God so loved the world that
He gave His only begotten Son,
that whoever believes in Him should not
perish but have everlasting life.*

John 3:16 NKJV

*This is an important Bible verse about God's love
for you. Practice saying this verse several times.
And then, talk to your mom or dad about exactly
what the verse means . . .*

A TIP FOR PARENTS

Today, talk to your child about . . . God's infinite love.

TODAY'S PRAYER

Dear Lord, the Bible teaches me that You are love.
And, I know that You love me. I will accept Your
love–and share it–this day and every day. Amen

DAY 47

GOD HAS A PLAN FOR YOU

We can make our plans, but the LORD determines our steps.

Proverbs 16:9 NLT

God has a plan for you. But God's plan may not always happen in the way that you would like or at the time of your own choosing. Still, God always knows best. Sometimes, even though you may want something very badly, you must still be patient and wait for the right time to get it. And the right time, of course, is determined by God. So trust Him always, obey Him always, and wait for Him to show you His plans. And that's exactly what He will do.

A VERY VEGGIE BRIGHT IDEA

God isn't a talent scout looking for someone who is "good enough" or "strong enough." He is looking for someone with a heart set on Him, and He will do the rest.

Vance Havner

TODAY'S PRAYER

Dear Lord, You have a wonderful plan for my life. Let me discover that plan and follow it so that I can be the person You want me to become. Amen

DAY 48

Honoring Jesus

If your life honors the name of Jesus, he will honor you.

2 Thessalonians 1:12 MSG

There's really no way around it: if you want to know God, you need to know His Son. And that's good, because getting to know Jesus can—and should—be a wonderful experience.

Jesus has an amazing love for you, so welcome Him into your heart today. When you do, you'll always be grateful that you did.

A VERY VEGGIE BRIGHT IDEA

The crucial question for each of us is this: What do you think of Jesus, and do you yet have a personal acquaintance with Him?

Hannah Whitall Smith

TODAY'S PRAYER

Dear Lord, thank You for Your Son, Jesus. Jesus is my friend, and I will try to know Him better this day and every day. Amen

DAY 49

VERY BIG IDEAS ABOUT JESUS

To start your day, take a few minutes to talk to your mom or dad about what these two quotations mean.

There is not a single thing that Jesus cannot change, control, and conquer because He is the living Lord.

Franklin Graham

This is my song through endless ages: Jesus led me all the way.

Fanny Crosby

TODAY'S PRAYER

Dear Lord, You sent Jesus to save the world. You sent Him so that I can live forever in heaven. Thank You for Your Son. I will follow Him, now and forever. Amen

DAY 50

Jesus is Your Very Best Friend!

Then Jesus said, "I am the bread that gives life. Whoever comes to me will never be hungry, and whoever believes in me will never be thirsty."

John 6:35 NCV

Who's the best friend any boy has ever had? And who's the best friend the whole world has ever had? Jesus, of course! When you invite Him into your heart, Jesus will be your friend, too . . . your friend forever.

Jesus has offered to share the gifts of everlasting life and everlasting love with the world . . . and with you. If you make mistakes, He'll still be your friend. If you behave badly, He'll still love you. If you feel sorry or sad, He can help you feel better.

Jesus wants you to have a happy, healthy life. He wants you to be generous and kind. He wants you to follow His example. And the rest is up to you. You can do it! And with a friend like Jesus, you will.

TODAY'S PRAYER

Dear Lord, Jesus loves me. Let me share His love with others so that through me, they can understand what it means to follow Him. Amen

DAY 51

SETTING THE RIGHT KIND OF EXAMPLE

Set an example of good works yourself, with integrity and dignity in your teaching.

Titus 2:7 HCSB

The Bible says that you are "the light that gives light to the world." The Bible also says that you should live in a way that lets other people understand what it means to be a good person. And of course, learning to share is an important part of being a good person.

What kind of "light" have you been giving off? Hopefully, you have been a good example for everybody to see. Why? Because the world needs all the light it can get, and that includes your light, too!

A TIP TO START YOUR DAY

Think about the ways that your behavior impacts your family and friends.

TODAY'S PRAYER

Dear Lord, let my light shine brightly for You. Let me be a positive example for all to see, and let me share love and kindness with my family and friends, now and always. Amen

DAY 52

IF YOU'RE TRYING TO BE PERFECT

The Lord says, "Forget what happened before, and do not think about the past. Look at the new thing I am going to do. It is already happening. Don't you see it? I will make a road in the desert and rivers in the dry land."

Isaiah 43:18-19 NCV

I f you're trying to be perfect, you're trying to do something that's impossible. No matter how much you try, you can't be a perfect person . . . and that's okay.

God doesn't expect you to live a mistake-free life–and neither should you. In the game of life, God expects you to try, but He doesn't always expect you to win. Sometimes, you'll make mistakes, but even then, you shouldn't give up!

So remember this: you don't have to be perfect to be a wonderful person. In fact, you don't even need to be "almost-perfect." You simply must try your best and leave the rest up to God.

TODAY'S PRAYER

Dear Lord, help me remember that I don't have to be perfect. I'll try hard to be a good person, Lord, but I won't expect to a perfect person. Amen

DAY 53

RESPECTING OTHERS

Just as you want others to do for you, do the same for them.

Luke 6:31 HCSB

How should you treat other people? Jesus has the answer to that question. Jesus wants you to treat other people exactly like you want to be treated: with kindness, respect, and courtesy. When you do, you'll make your family and friends happy . . . and that's what God wants.

So if you're wondering how to treat someone else, follow the Golden Rule: treat the other people like you want them to treat you. When you do, you'll be obeying your Father in heaven and you'll be making other folks happy at the same time.

A TIP TO START YOUR DAY

When dealing with other people, it is important to try to walk in their shoes.

TODAY'S PRAYER

Dear Lord, help me always to do my very best to treat others as I wish to be treated. The Golden Rule is Your rule, Father. I will make it my rule, too. Amen

DAY 54

IT'S GOOD TO HAVE GOOD HABITS

Do not be deceived: "Evil company corrupts good habits."

1 Corinthians 15:33 NKJV

Most boys have a few habits they'd like to change, and maybe you do, too. If so, God can help.

If you trust God, and if you keep asking Him to help you change bad habits, He will help you make yourself into a new person. So, if at first you don't succeed, keep praying. God is listening, and He's ready to help you be a better person if you ask Him . . . so ask Him!

A TIP TO START YOUR DAY

The old saying is familiar and true: "First you make your habits; then your habits make you." So it's always a good time to ask this question: "What kind of person are my habits making me?"

TODAY'S PRAYER

Dear Lord, today I'm asking for Your help. Please help me do things that are pleasing to You, and help me form habits that are pleasing to You.

DAY 55

The Best Excuse is No Excuse

Each of us will be rewarded for his own hard work.

1 Corinthians 3:8 TLB

What is an excuse? Well, when you make up an excuse, that means that you try to come up with a good reason that you didn't do something that you should have done.

Anybody can make up excuses, and you can too. But you shouldn't get into the habit of making too many excuses. Why? Because excuses don't work. And why don't they work? Because everybody has already heard so many excuses that almost everybody can recognize excuses when they hear them.

So the next time you're tempted to make up an excuse, don't. Instead of making an excuse, do what you think is right. After all, the very best excuse of all . . . is no excuse.

A TIP TO START YOUR DAY

Making up a string of excuses is usually harder than doing the work.

TODAY'S PRAYER

Dear Lord, when I'm tempted to make excuses, help me be strong as I accept responsibility for my actions. Amen

DAY 56

YOU'LL FEEL BETTER WHEN YOU FORGIVE OTHER PEOPLE

A wise person is patient. He will be honored if he ignores a wrong done against him.

Proverbs 19:11 ICB

Is forgiving someone else an easy thing for you to do or a hard thing? If you're like most people, forgiving others can be hard, Hard, HARD! But even if you're having a very hard time forgiving someone, you can do it if you talk things over with your parents, and if you talk things over with God.

Do you find forgiveness difficult? Talk about it and pray about it. You'll feel better when you do.

TODAY'S PRAYER

Dear Lord, even when forgiveness is hard, help me be a person who forgives other people, just as You have forgiven me. Amen

Sometimes, it's important to Slow Down

Don't burn out; keep yourselves fueled and aflame. Be alert servants of the Master, cheerfully expectant. Don't quit in hard times; pray all the harder.

Romans 12:11-12 MSG

Everybody knows you're a very busy boy. But here's a question: Are you able to squeeze time into your schedule for God? Hopefully so!

Nothing is more important than the time you spend with your Heavenly Father. So take some time today and every day to pray and to thank God for His blessings. God will be glad you did, and you'll be glad, too.

TODAY'S PRAYER

Dear Lord, I have lots of things to do, but nothing I do is more important than the time I spend with You. I thank You, Lord, for Your blessings, for Your Son, and for Your Bible. I will take time to read it every day. Amen

DAY 58

Church is important

For where two or three are gathered together in My name, I am there among them.

Matthew 18:20 HCSB

When your parents take you to church, are you pleased to go? Hopefully so. After all, church is a wonderful place to learn about God's rules.

The church belongs to God just as surely as you belong to God. That's why the church is a good place to learn about God and about His Son, Jesus.

So when your mom and dad take you to church, remember this: church is a fine place to be . . . and you're lucky to be there.

A TIP TO START YOUR DAY

If somebody starts making up reasons not to go to church, don't pay any attention . . . even if that person is you!

TODAY'S PRAYER

Dear Lord, I thank You for Your church. When I am in church, I will behave myself and I will learn about Your promises. And when I leave church, I will carry Your message into the world. Amen

DAY 59

TRY TO MEMORIZE THIS VERSE

This is the day the LORD has made;
let us rejoice and be glad in it.

Psalm 118:24 NIV

This is an important Bible verse about being joyful.
Practice saying this verse several times. And then,
talk to your mom or dad about exactly what it
means . . .

A TIP FOR PARENTS
Today, talk to your child about . . .
the need to celebrate the gift of life.

TODAY'S PRAYER
Dear Lord, You have given me this wonderful
day, and I will celebrate the life You have given
me. Amen

DAY 60

FORGIVE QUICKLY AND APOLOGIZE QUICKLY

Be even-tempered, content with second place, quick to forgive an offense. Forgive as quickly and completely as the Master forgave you. And regardless of what else you put on, wear love. It's your basic, all-purpose garment. Never be without it.

Colossians 3:13-14 MSG

When you make a mistake or hurt someone's feelings, what should you do? You should say you're sorry and ask for forgiveness. And you should do so sooner, not later.

The longer you wait to apologize, the harder it is on you. So if you've done something wrong, don't be afraid to ask for forgiveness, and don't be afraid to ask for it NOW!

A TIP TO START YOUR DAY

Forgiving other people is one way of strengthening your relationship with God . . .

TODAY'S PRAYER

Dear Lord, when I make a mistake, help me be quick to admit it and quick to ask for forgiveness. Amen

DAY 61

Good Friends are a Very Good Thing to Have

If you've gotten anything at all out of following Christ, if his love has made any difference in your life, if being in a community of the Spirit means anything to you, if you have a heart, if you care–then do me a favor: Agree with each other, love each other, be deep-spirited friends.

Philippians 2:1-2 MSG

The Bible tells us that friendship can be a wonderful thing. That's why it's good to know how to make and to keep good friends.

If you want to make lots of friends, practice the Golden Rule with everybody you know. Be kind. Share. Say nice things. Be helpful. When you do, you'll discover that the Golden Rule isn't just a nice way to behave; it's also a great way to make and to keep friends!

TODAY'S PRAYER

Lord, thank You for my friends. Let me be a trustworthy friend to others, and let my love for You be shown by my genuine love for them. Amen

Little White Lies aren't as Small as They Look

Doing what is right brings freedom to honest people.

Proverbs 11:6 ICB

Sometimes, people convince themselves that it's okay to tell "little white lies." Sometimes people convince themselves that itsy bitsy lies aren't harmful. But there's a problem: little lies have a way of growing into big ones, and once they grow up, they cause lots of problems.

Remember that lies, no matter what size, are not part of God's plan for our lives, so tell the truth about everything. It's the right thing to do, and besides: when you always tell the truth, you don't have to try and remember what you said!

TODAY'S PRAYER

Dear Lord, help me to make decisions that are pleasing to You. Help me to be honest, patient, and kind. And help me to follow the teachings of Jesus, not just tomorrow, but every day. Amen

DAY 63

YOUR SPECIAL FRIENDSHIP WITH JESUS

I am the Vine, you are the branches. When you're joined with me and I with you, the relation intimate and organic, the harvest is sure to be abundant.

John 15:5 MSG

Whether you realize it or not, you already have a relationship with Jesus. Hopefully, it's a close relationship! Why? Because the friendship you form with Jesus will help you every day of your life . . . and beyond!

You can either choose to invite Him into your heart, or you can ignore Him altogether. Welcome Him today–and while you're at it, encourage your friends and family members to do the same.

TODAY'S PRAYER

Dear Jesus, I know that You love me today and that You will love me forever. And, I thank You for Your love . . . today and forever. Amen

DAY 64

Laughter is a Gift

There is a time for everything, and everything on earth has its special season. There is a time to cry and a time to laugh. There is a time to be sad and a time to dance.

Ecclesiastes 3:1, 4 NCV

Do you like to laugh? Of course you do! Laughter is a gift from God that He hopes you'll use in the right way. So here are a few things to remember: 1. God wants you to be happy. 2. Laughter is a good thing when you're laughing at the right things. 3. You should laugh with people, but you should never laugh at them.

God created laughter for a reason . . . and God knows best. So do yourself a favor: laugh at the right things . . . and laugh a lot!

TODAY'S PRAYER

Dear Lord, laughter is Your gift to me; help me to enjoy it. Every day, Father, put a smile on my face, and help me to share that smile with my family and my friends. Amen

DAY 65

Be Respectful

Show respect for all people. Love the brothers and sisters of God's family.

1 Peter 2:17 ICB

Are you the kind of boy who's polite and respectful to your parents and teachers? And do you do your best to treat everybody with the respect they deserve? If you want to obey God's rules, then you should be able to answer yes to these questions.

Remember this: the Bible teaches you to be a respectful person—and if it's right there in the Bible, it's certainly the right thing to do!

A TIP TO START YOUR DAY

If you're angry with your mom or your dad, don't blurt out something unkind. If you can't say anything nice, go to your room and don't come out until you can.

TODAY'S PRAYER

Dear Lord, please give me the maturity to respect my teachers, my coaches, and my parents. Amen

DAY 66

VERY BIG IDEAS ABOUT GOD'S GIFTS

To start your day, take a few minutes to talk to your mom or dad about what these two quotations mean.

God is the giver, and we are the receivers. And His richest gifts are bestowed not upon those who do the greatest things, but upon those who accept His abundance and His grace.

Hannah Whitall Smith

God never turns away from the sincere heart.

Max Lucado

TODAY'S PRAYER

Dear Lord, I thank You for the many gifts You have given me and my family. I will do my best to use those gifts, Lord. And I will help my family use theirs. Amen

DAY 67

GOD'S POWER

I pray . . . that you may know . . . his uncomparably great power for us who believe. . . .

Ephesians 1:18-19 NIV

How strong is God? Stronger than anybody can imagine! But even if we can't understand God's power, we can respect His power. And we can be sure that God has the strength to guide us and protect us forever.

The next time you're worried or afraid, remember this: if God is powerful enough to create the universe and everything in it, He's also strong enough to take care of you. Now that's a comforting thought!

A VERY VEGGIE BRIGHT IDEA

The power of God through His Spirit will work within us to the degree that we permit it.

Mrs. Charles E. Cowman

TODAY'S PRAYER

Dear God, Your power is far too great for me to understand. But I can sense Your presence and Your love every day of my life—and that's exactly what I will try to do! Amen

DAY 68

Very Big ideas about Obedience

To start your day, take a few minutes to talk to your mom or dad about what these two quotations mean.

You may not always see immediate results, but all God wants is your obedience and faithfulness.

Vonette Bright

Although God causes all things to work together for good for His children, He still holds us accountable for our behavior.

Kay Arthur

TODAY'S PRAYER

Dear Lord, I thank You for the rules You have given me. And I understand that the best way to say "thank You" is to obey those rules every day. Amen

DAY 69

SLOW DOWN!

Knowing God leads to self-control. Self-control leads to patient endurance, and patient endurance leads to godliness.

2 Peter 1:6 NLT

Maybe you're one of those boys who try to do everything fast, faster, or fastest! If so, maybe you sometimes do things before you think about the consequences of your actions. If that's the case, it's probably a good idea to slow down a little bit so you can think before you act. When you do, you'll soon discover the value of thinking carefully about things before you get started. And while you're at it, it's probably a good idea to think before you speak, too. After all, you'll never have to apologize for something that you didn't say.

TODAY'S PRAYER

Dear Lord, tomorrow and every day after that, I will slow down and think about things before I do them. And when I slow down to think about things, I will always try to do what's right. Amen

DAY 70

Very Big ideas about God's Love

To start your day, take a few minutes to talk to your mom or dad about what these two quotations mean.

The love of God is revealed in that He laid down His life for His enemies.

Oswald Chambers

When once we are assured that God is good, then there can be nothing left to fear.

Hannah Whitall Smith

TODAY'S PRAYER

Dear God, the Bible teaches me that Your love lasts forever. Thank You, God, for Your love. Let me trust Your promises, and let me live according to Your teachings now and forever. Amen

DAY 71

DON'T WORRY; TRUST GOD!

The Lord himself will go before you. He will be with you; he will not leave you or forget you. Don't be afraid and don't worry.

Deuteronomy 31:8 NCV

It's easy to worry about things–big things and little things. But the Bible promises us that if we learn to trust God more and more each day, we won't worry so much.

Are you worried about something? If so, try doing these two things: First, ask God for His help. Second, talk things over with your parents. When you do these things, you won't worry so much. And that's good . . . VERY good!

A TIP TO START YOUR DAY

Worried about something you said or did? If you made a mistake yesterday, the day to fix it is today. Then, you won't have to worry about it tomorrow.

TODAY'S PRAYER

Dear Lord, when I'm discouraged or afraid, I can always talk to You and to my parents. I thank You for Your love, Father . . . and I thank You for my family. Amen

DAY 72

iT Pays To Be HeLPFuL

Work at getting along with each other and with God. Otherwise you'll never get so much as a glimpse of God.

Helping other people can be fun! When you help others, you feel better about yourself—and you'll know that God approves of what you're doing.

When you learn how to cooperate with your family and friends, you'll soon discover that it's more fun when everybody works together.

So do everybody a favor: learn better ways to share and better ways to cooperate. It's the right thing to do.

A TIP TO START YOUR DAY

Cooperation pays. When you cooperate with your friends and family, you'll feel good about yourself—and your family and friends will feel good about you, too.

TODAY'S PRAYER

Dear Lord, help me learn to be kind, courteous, and cooperative with my family and with my friends. Amen

SHARE YOUR BLESSINGS

Remember this: the person who sows sparingly will also reap sparingly, and the person who sows generously will also reap generously.

2 Corinthians 9:6 HCSB

Jesus told us that we should be generous with other people, but sometimes we don't feel much like sharing. Instead of sharing the things that we have, we want to keep them all to ourselves. But God doesn't want selfishness to rule our hearts; He wants us to be generous.

Are you lucky enough to have nice things? If so, God's instructions are clear: you must share your blessings with others. And that's exactly the way it should be. After all, think how generous God has been with you.

TODAY'S PRAYER

Dear Lord, help me be a generous and cheerful person. Let me be kind to those who need my smile, and let me share with those who need my help. Amen

DAY 74

GOD'S NEVER-ENDING LOVE

The unfailing love of the Lord never ends!

Lamentations 3:22 NLT

How much does God love you? He loves you so much that He sent His Son, Jesus, to come to this earth for you! And, when you accept Jesus into your heart, God gives you a gift that is more precious than gold: that gift is called "eternal life," which means that you will live forever with God in heaven!

God's love is bigger and more powerful than anybody can imagine, but it is very real. So do yourself a favor right now: accept God's love with open arms and welcome His Son, Jesus, into your heart. When you do, your life will be changed today, tomorrow, and forever.

TODAY'S PRAYER

Dear God, I know that Your love lasts forever. I thank You, Father, for Your amazing love. Every day, I will share Your love with others, and I will do my best to walk in the footsteps of Your Son. Amen

DAY 75

Very Big ideas About Wisdom

To start your day, take a few minutes to talk to your mom or dad about what these two quotations mean.

If we neglect the Bible, we cannot expect to benefit from the wisdom and direction that result from knowing God's Word.

Vonette Bright

If you lack knowledge, go to school. If you lack wisdom, get on your knees.

Vance Havner

TODAY'S PRAYER

Dear Lord, let me be an understanding person, especially to my family and friends. Let me be kind to those who need my encouragement and let me be a helpful, generous Christian now and always. Amen

DAY 76

When Nobody is Watching

Moderation is better than muscle, self-control better than political power.

Proverbs 16:32 MSG

When your teachers or parents aren't watching, what should you do? The answer, of course, is that you should behave exactly like you would if they were watching you. But sometimes, you may be tempted to do otherwise.

When a parent steps away or a teacher looks away, you may be tempted to say something or do something that you would not do if they were standing right beside you. But remember this: when nobody's watching, it's up to you to control yourself. And that's exactly what everybody wants you to do: your teachers want you to control yourself, and so do your parents. And so, by the way, does God.

TODAY'S PRAYER

Dear Lord, the Bible teaches me to be smart, not foolish. So help me slow down and think things through so I can make better decisions and fewer mistakes. Amen

it's important to Share

In every way I've shown you that by laboring like this, it is necessary to help the weak and to keep in mind the words of the Lord Jesus, for He said, "It is more blessed to give than to receive."

Acts 20:35 HCSB

A re you one of those boys who is lucky enough to have a closet filled up with stuff? If so, it's probably time to share some of it.

When your mom or dad says it's time to clean up your closet and give some things away, don't be sad. Instead of whining, think about all the children who could enjoy the things that you don't use very much. And while you're at it, think about what Jesus might tell you to do if He were here. Jesus would tell you to share generously and cheerfully. And that's exactly what you should do!

TODAY'S PRAYER

Dear Lord, You've given so much to my family and to me. And there are so many people in this world who need so much. Help me to be generous now and forever. Amen

Very Big ideas about Going to Church

To start your day, take a few minutes to talk to your mom or dad about what these two quotations mean.

The church needs people who are doers of the Word and not just hearers.

Warren Wiersbe

The first place of Christian service for any Christian is in a local church.

Jerry Clower

TODAY'S PRAYER

Dear Lord, thank You for my church. When I am at church, I will be generous, kind, well-behaved, and respectful. And when I am not at church, I will act the same way. Amen

Be Joyful and Hopeful

Make me hear joy and gladness.

Psalm 51:8 NKJV

Hope is a very good thing to have . . . and to share. So make this promise to yourself and keep it: promise yourself that you'll be a hopeful person. Think good thoughts. Trust God. Become friends with Jesus. And trust your hopes, not your fears. Then, when you've filled your heart with hope and gladness, share your good thoughts with friends. They'll be better for it, and so will you.

A TIP TO START YOUR DAY

Think about all the things you have (starting with your family and your faith) . . . and think about all the things you can do! Believe in yourself.

TODAY'S PRAYER

Dear Lord, I have so many reasons to be happy. Let me think good thoughts and look for the good in other people. And, help me be a joyful person now and always. Amen

DAY 80

GOD WANTS YOU TO SHARE

I will make you into a great nation and I will bless you; I will make your name great, and you will be a blessing. I will bless those who bless you, and whoever curses you I will curse; and all peoples on earth will be blessed through you.

Genesis 12:2-3 NIV

You've heard it plenty of times from your parents and teachers: share your things. But it's important to realize that sharing isn't just something that grown-ups want you to do. It's also something that God wants you to do, too.

The word "possessions" is another way of describing the stuff that belongs to you. Your clothes, your toys, your books, and things like that are "your possessions."

Jesus says that you should learn how to share your possessions without feeling bad about it. Sometimes, of course, it's very hard to share and very easy to be stingy. But God wants you to share–and to keep sharing!

TODAY'S PRAYER

Dear Lord, help me to learn the importance of sharing. The Bible teaches me to share, and so do my parents. Now, it's up to me to learn how to share the things that I have–and it's up to me to share kind words and good deeds with my family and friends. Amen

DAY 81

Making Things Better

For out of the overflow of the heart the mouth speaks.

Matthew 12:34 NIV

When we're frustrated or tired, it's easier to speak first and think second. But that's not the best way to talk to other people. The Bible tells us that "a good person's words will help many others." But if our words are to be helpful, we must put some thought into them.

The next time you're tempted to say something unkind, remember that your words can and should be helpful to others, not hurtful. God wants to use you to make this world a better place, and He will use the things that you say to help accomplish that goal . . . if you let Him.

A TIP TO START YOUR DAY

Words have the power to encourage or discourage others. So watch what you say.

TODAY'S PRAYER

Dear Lord, You hear every word that I say. Help me remember to speak words that are honest, kind, and helpful. Amen

DAY 82

Learning to Control Yourself

But endurance must do its complete work, so that you may be mature and complete, lacking nothing.

James 1:4 HCSB

I f you're having trouble learning how to control your actions or your emotions, you're not alone! Most people have problems with self-control from time to time, so don't be discouraged. Just remember that self-control requires practice and lots of it. So if you're a little discouraged, don't give up. Just keep working on improving your self-control until you get better at it . . . and if you keep trying, you can be sure that sooner or later you will get better at it.

A TIP TO START YOUR DAY

If you learn to control yourself, you'll be glad. If you can't learn to control yourself, you'll be sad.

TODAY'S PRAYER

Dear Lord, there are things that You want me to do right now. So, Father, help me finish the things that you want me to do. Amen

DAY 83

Very Big ideas about What Happens When you Pray

To start your day, take a few minutes to talk to your mom or dad about what these two quotations mean.

Prayer succeeds when all else fails.

E. M. Bounds

Prayer accomplishes more than anything else.

Bill Bright

TODAY'S PRAYER

Dear Lord, help me remember the importance of prayer. You always hear my prayers, God; let me always pray them! Amen

Patience and Peace

I leave you peace. My peace I give you. I do not give it to you as the world does. So don't let your hearts be troubled.

John 14:27 ICB

Patience and peace go together. And the words from John 14:27 remind us that Jesus offers us peace, not as the world gives, but as He alone gives. We, as believers, can accept His peace or ignore it. When we accept the peace of Jesus Christ into our hearts, our lives are changed forever, and we become more loving, patient Christians.

Christ's peace is offered freely; it has already been paid for; it is ours for the asking. So let us ask . . . and then share.

TODAY'S PRAYER

Dear Lord, when I am impatient, slow me down and let me think before I say things or do things. Teach me patience, Lord, so that I can become the kind of person You want me to be. Amen

Staying Out of Trouble

Don't envy bad people; don't even want to be around them. All they think about is causing a disturbance; all they talk about is making trouble.

Proverbs 24:1-2 MSG

One way that you can feel better about yourself is by staying out of trouble. And one way that you can stay out of trouble is by making friends with people who, like you, want to do what's right.

Are your friends the kind of kids who encourage you to behave yourself? If so, you've chosen your friends wisely. But if your friends try to get you in trouble, perhaps it's time to think long and hard about making some new friends.

Whether you know it or not, you're probably going to behave like your friends behave. So pick out friends who make you want to behave better, not worse. When you do, you'll feel better about yourself.

TODAY'S PRAYER

Dear Lord, when my friends misbehave, it's easy to join them. But I must remember, Father, that I must follow Your Son every day. And if my friends misbehave, I should never join them. Amen

DAY 86

FORGIVENESS MEANS
CHANGING YOUR HEART

Whoever forgives someone's sin makes a friend, but gossiping about the sin breaks up friendships.

Proverbs 17:9 NCV

What does it mean to forgive? Forgiveness means that you decide to change your angry thoughts into kind thoughts. Forgiveness means that you decide not to stay mad at somebody who has done something wrong. Forgiveness happens when you decide that obeying God is more important than staying angry.

Sometimes forgiveness can be very hard, but it's the right thing to do. Why? Because forgiveness is God's way, and you should make it your way, too!

A VERY VEGGIE BRIGHT IDEA

We cannot be right with God until we are right with one another.

Charles Swindoll

TODAY'S PRAYER

Dear Lord, whenever I am angry, give me a forgiving heart. And help me remember that the best day to forgive somebody is this one. Amen

DAY 87

IT'S BETTER TO SHARE

If you have two shirts, share with the person who does not have one. If you have food, share that too.

Luke 3:11 ICB

How many times have you heard someone say, "Don't touch that; it's mine!" If you're like most of us, you've heard those words many times and you may have even said them yourself.

The Bible tells us that it's better for us to share things than it is to keep them all to ourselves. And the Bible also tells us that when we share, it's best to do so cheerfully. So be sure to share. It's the best way because it's God's way.

TODAY'S PRAYER

Dear Lord, help me to learn the importance of sharing. The Bible teaches me to share, and so do my parents. Now, it's up to me to learn how to share the things that I have—and it's up to me to share kind words and good deeds with my family and friends. Amen

DAY 88

TRY TO MEMORIZE THIS VERSE

*For to me to live is Christ,
and to die is gain.*

Philippians 1:21 KJV

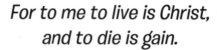

*Here's a Bible verse worth remembering!
Practice saying it several times.
And then, talk to your mom or dad about
exactly what the verse means . . .*

A TIP FOR PARENTS

Today, talk to your child about . . . living for Christ.

TODAY'S PRAYER

Dear Lord, tomorrow and every day after that, I will do my best to walk in the footsteps of Your Son. I thank You, Father, for Jesus, and for the life that I will share with Him forever in heaven. Amen

DAY 89

WHAT KIND OF EXAMPLE ARE YOU?

You are young, but do not let anyone treat you as if you were not important. Be an example to show the believers how they should live. Show them with your words, with the way you live, with your love, with your faith, and with your pure life.

1 Timothy 4:12 ICB

L ike it or not, your behavior is a powerful example to others. The question is not whether you will be an example to your friends; the only question is this: What kind of example will you be?

Corrie ten Boom advised, "Don't worry about what you do not understand. Worry about what you do understand in the Bible but do not live by." And that's good advice because your family and friends are always watching . . . and so, for that matter, is God.

TODAY'S PRAYER

Lord, I want to be a good example to my friends and family. So help me say things and do things that show everybody what it means to be a Christian. Amen

DAY 90

GOD SEES YOUR GOOD DEEDS

A good person produces good deeds from a good heart, and an evil person produces evil deeds from an evil heart. Whatever is in your heart determines what you say.

Luke 6:45 NLT

It's good to do good deeds. Even when nobody's watching, God is. And God knows whether you've done the right thing or the wrong thing.

So if you're tempted to misbehave when nobody is looking, remember this: there is never a time when "nobody's watching." Somebody is always watching over you—and that Somebody, of course, is your Father in heaven. Don't let Him down!

TODAY'S PRAYER

Dear Lord, when my family or friends need my help, remind me to behave myself like the Good Samaritan. Let me be generous, kind, and helpful, Lord, today, tomorrow, and every day of my life. Amen

DAY 91

iF You Make a MistaKe

Therefore, if anyone is in Christ, he is a new creation; the old has gone, the new has come!

2 Corinthians 5:17 NIV

Mistakes: nobody likes 'em but everybody makes 'em. And you're no different! When you make mistakes (and you will), you should do your best to correct them, to learn from them, and to pray for the wisdom to avoid those same mistakes in the future.

If you want to become smarter faster, you'll learn from your mistakes the first time you make them. When you do, that means that you won't keep making the same mistakes over and over again, and that's the smart way to live.

TODAY'S PRAYER

Dear Lord, everybody makes mistakes, including me. When I make a mistake, help me learn something and help me forgive myself. I want to keep learning things every day, and when I learn from my mistakes, it helps me become a better person. Thank You, Lord, for the chance to learn. Amen

DAY 92

Make Sure You're a Good Example to Your Friends

We have around us many people whose lives tell us what faith means. So let us run the race that is before us and never give up. We should remove from our lives anything that would get in the way and the sin that so easily holds us back.

Hebrews 12:1 NCV

A re you a boy whose behavior serves as a good example for other kids? If so, congratulations! God smiles upon people (like you) who do what's right, but that's not all. God also rewards good behavior when He sees it (and you can be sure that He sees it!).

So, do yourself and your friends a favor: do the right thing every chance you get.

A TIP TO START YOUR DAY

The best example is Jesus. If you're not sure what to do, ask yourself what He would do.

TODAY'S PRAYER

Dear Lord, I will do my best to follow in the footsteps of Your Son. Jesus is Your gift to the world. Please let others see Him through me. Amen

DAY 93

Forgive and Forget

And forgive us our sins, for we ourselves also forgive everyone in debt to us.

Luke 11:4 HCSB

Have you heard the saying "Forgive and forget"? Well, it's certainly easier said than done. It's easy to talk about forgiving somebody, but actually forgiving that person can be much harder to do. And when it comes to forgetting, forget about it!

Sometimes, it's impossible to forget the people who hurt our feelings. But even if we can't forget, we can forgive. And that's exactly what God teaches us to do.

A TIP TO START YOUR DAY

Sometimes, you may forgive someone once and then, at a later time, become angry at the very same person again. If so, you must forgive that person again and again . . . until it sticks!

TODAY'S PRAYER

Dear Lord, when somebody hurts my feelings, let me be patient and kind. And when a friend does something wrong, help me do the right thing by offering my forgiveness sooner rather than later! Amen

FORGIVING OTHER PEOPLE CAN BE HARD, BUT IT'S WORTH IT

Smart people know how to hold their tongue; their grandeur is to forgive and forget.

Proverbs 19:11 MSG

Forgiving other people requires practice and lots of it. So when it comes to forgiveness, here's something you should remember: if at first you don't succeed, don't give up!

Are you having trouble forgiving someone (or, for that matter, forgiving yourself for a mistake that you've made)? If so, remember that forgiveness isn't easy, so keep trying until you get it right . . . and if you keep trying, you can be sure that sooner or later, you will get it right.

A TIP TO START YOUR DAY

For most of us–kids and grown-ups alike–forgiveness doesn't come naturally. Keep practicing until it does.

TODAY'S PRAYER

Dear Lord, please help me forgive other people. You have forgiven me. Now, it's my turn to forgive others. Amen

DAY 95

TRY TO MEMORIZE THIS VERSE

For where two or three
are gathered together in My name,
I am there among them.

Matthew 18:20 HCSB

These are words that Jesus spoke.
Practice saying this verse several times.
And then, talk to your mom or dad about
exactly what the verse means . . .

A TIP FOR PARENTS

Today, talk to your child about . . . the presence of God.

TODAY'S PRAYER

Dear Lord, You are always with me, and You
are always listening. Thank You, Lord, for Your
love, for Your power, and for Your Son. Amen

DAY 96

Today is a Wonderful Day to Be Happy

But happy are those . . . whose hope is in the LORD their God.

Psalm 146:5 NLT

If we could decide to be happy "once and for all," life would be so much simpler, but it doesn't seem to work that way. If we want happiness to last, we need to create good thoughts every day that we live. Yesterday's good thoughts don't count . . . we've got to think more good thoughts now.

Each new day is a gift from God, so treat it that way. Think about it like this: today is another wonderful chance to celebrate God's gifts.

So celebrate–starting now–and keep celebrating forever!

TODAY'S PRAYER

Dear Lord, You have given me so many reasons to be happy. Every day, I will try to be a joyful Christian, as I give thanks for Your gifts, for Your love, and for Your Son. Amen

DAY 97

Honesty Begins on the Inside

In every way be an example of doing good deeds. When you teach, do it with honesty and seriousness.

Titus 2:7 NCV

Where does honesty begin? In your own heart and your own head. If you sincerely want to be an honest person, then you must ask God to help you find the courage and the determination to be honest all of the time.

Honesty is not a "sometimes" thing. If you intend to be a truthful person, you must make truthfulness a habit that becomes so much a part of you that you don't have to decide whether or not you're going to tell the truth. Instead, you will simply tell the truth because it's the kind of person you are.

Lying is an easy habit to fall into, and a terrible one. So make up your mind that you're going to be an honest person, and then stick to your decision. That's what your parents want you to do, and that's what God wants, too. And since they love you more than you know, trust them.

TODAY'S PRAYER

Dear Lord, I know that it's important to be an honest person. Since I want other people to be truthful with me, let me be truthful with them, today and every day. Amen

DAY 98

GOOD FRIENDS BEHAVE THEMSELVES

As iron sharpens iron, so people can improve each other.

Proverbs 27:17 NCV

O ur world is filled with pressures: some good, some bad. The pressures that we feel to follow God's rules are the good kind of pressures (and the friends who make us want to obey God are good friends). But sometimes, we may feel pressure to misbehave, pressure from friends who want us to disobey the rules.

If you want to please God and your parents, make friends with people who behave themselves. When you do, you'll be much more likely to behave yourself, too . . . and that's a very good thing.

A TIP TO START YOUR DAY

Remember: if you choose friends who behave themselves, you'll be far more likely to behave yourself, too.

TODAY'S PRAYER

Dear Lord, the Bible says that if I choose friends who behave themselves well, they can help me become a better person. Help me choose my friends carefully, Father, now and always. Amen

You Can't Please Everybody

My son, if sinners entice you, don't be persuaded.

Proverbs 1:10 HCSB

Here's an important lesson you might as well learn today: you can't please everybody.

Are you one of those boys who tries to please just about everybody in sight? If so, you'd better watch out! After all, if you worry too much about pleasing your friends, you may not worry enough about pleasing God.

Whom will you try to please tomorrow: your God or your friends? The answer to that question should be simple. Your first job is to obey God's rules . . . and that means obeying your parents, too!

So don't worry too much about pleasing your friends or neighbors. Try, instead, to please your heavenly Father and your parents. No exceptions.

TODAY'S PRAYER

Dear Lord, the Bible teaches me that pleasing people is not nearly as important as pleasing You. Let me please You, Lord, now and always. Amen

DAY 100

Let Your Parents Help

The one who lives with integrity is righteous; his children who come after him will be happy.

Proverbs 20:7 HCSB

Whenever you want to get better at something, you should always be willing to let your parents help out in any way they can. After all, your parents want you to become the very best person you can be. So, if you want to become better at controlling your own behavior, ask your parents to help. How can they help out? By reminding you to slow down and think about things before you do them–not after. It's as simple as that.

A TIP TO START YOUR DAY

Your parents love you and want to help you. Their job is to help . . . your job is to listen carefully to the things they say.

TODAY'S PRAYER

Dear God, I pray for those who care for me, especially my parents. Give them wisdom, courage, compassion, and faith. Amen

DAY 101

VERY BIG IDEAS ABOUT Heaven

To start your day, take a few minutes to talk to your mom or dad about what these two quotations mean.

Heaven is a place promised and prepared by Jesus for those who follow Him.

Bill Bright

One of these days, our Father will scoop us up in His strong arms and we will hear Him say those sweet and comforting words, "Come on, child. We're going home."

Gloria Gaither

TODAY'S PRAYER

Dear Lord, I thank You for the gift of eternal life that is mine through Your Son, Jesus. I will keep the promise of heaven in my heart every day of my life. Amen

Don't Play The Blame Game

People's own foolishness ruins their lives, but in their minds they blame the Lord.

Proverbs 19:3 NCV

When something goes wrong, do you look for somebody to blame? And do you try to blame other people even if you're the one who made the mistake? Hopefully not!

It's silly to try to blame other people for your own mistakes, so don't do it.

If you've done something you're ashamed of, don't look for somebody to blame; look for a way to say, "I'm sorry, and I won't make that same mistake again."

A TIP TO START YOUR DAY

It's very tempting to blame others when you make a mistake, but it's more honest to look in the mirror first.

TODAY'S PRAYER

Dear Lord, when I make a mistake, it's tempting to blame somebody else. But that's the wrong thing to do. Help me to accept responsibility for the mistakes I make. And help me learn from them. Amen

DAY 103

Sharing Makes You Feel Better About Yourself

God loves the person who gives happily.

2 Corinthians 9:7 ICB

When you learn to share your things, you'll know that you've done exactly what God wants you to do–and you'll feel better about yourself.

The Bible teaches that it's better to be generous than selfish. But sometimes, you won't feel like sharing your things, and you'll be tempted to keep everything for yourself. When you're feeling a little bit stingy, remember this: God wants you to share your things with people who need your help.

When you learn to be a more generous boy, God will be pleased with you . . . and you'll be pleased with yourself.

TODAY'S PRAYER

Dear Lord, I know there is no happiness in keeping Your blessings for myself. So, I will share my blessings with my family, with my friends, and with people who need my help. Amen

DAY 104

Know When To Say No

Wisdom will save you from the ways of wicked men. . . .

Proverbs 2:12 NIV

It happens to all of us at one time or another: a friend asks us to do something that we think is wrong. What should we do? Should we try to please our friend by doing something bad? No way! It's not worth it!

Trying to please our friends is okay. What's not okay is misbehaving in order to do so. Do you have a friend who encourages you to misbehave? Hopefully you don't have any friends like that. But if you do, say, "No, NO, NOOOOOO!" And what if your friend threatens to break up the friendship? Let him! Friendships like that just aren't worth it.

A TIP TO START YOUR DAY

Your family has rules . . . and it's better for everybody when you obey them.

TODAY'S PRAYER

Dear Lord, from now on I will worry less about pleasing other people and more about pleasing You. Amen

DAY 105

VERY BIG IDEAS ABOUT CHEERFULNESS

To start your day, take a few minutes to talk to your mom or dad about what these two quotations mean.

The people whom I have seen succeed best in life have always been cheerful and hopeful people who went about their business with a smile on their faces.

Charles Kingsley

When we bring sunshine into the lives of others, we're warmed by it ourselves. When we spill a little happiness, it splashes on us.

Barbara Johnson

TODAY'S PRAYER

Dear Lord, I have so many reasons to be cheerful. Help me be a joyful Christian, quick to laugh and slow to frown. Amen

DAY 106

PATIENCE AND LOVE

I wait for the Lord; I wait, and put my hope in His word.

Psalm 130:5 HCSB

The Bible tells us that God is love and that if we wish to know Him, we must have love in our hearts. Sometimes, of course, when we're tired, angry, or frustrated, it is very hard for us to be loving. Thankfully, anger and frustration are feelings that come and go, but God's love lasts forever.

If you'd like to become a more patient boy, talk to God in prayer, listen to what He says, and share His love with your family and friends. God is always listening, and He's ready to talk to you . . . now!

A TIP TO START YOUR DAY

God has been patient with you . . . now it's your turn to be patient with others.

TODAY'S PRAYER

Dear Lord, sometimes I am not as patient as I should be. Slow me down, Lord, and teach me patience. Amen

Sometimes it's Hard to Be Honest . . . But it's always Right

It is better to be poor and honest than to be foolish and tell lies.

Proverbs 19:1 ICB

Telling the truth can be hard sometimes. But even when telling the truth is very hard, that's exactly what you should do. If you're afraid to tell the truth, pray to God for the courage to do the right thing, and then do it!

If you've ever told a big lie, and then had to live with the big consequences of that lie, you know that it's far more trouble to tell a lie than it is to tell the truth. But lies aren't just troubling to us; they're also troubling to God! So tell the truth, even when it's hard to do; you'll be glad you did . . . and so will He!

TODAY'S PRAYER

Dear Lord, help me be a person whose words are true and whose heart is pure. In everything that I do, let me use Jesus as my model and my guide. Amen

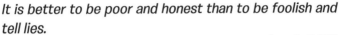

DAY 108

God Has Answers

For I know the thoughts that I think toward you, says the Lord, thoughts of peace and not of evil, to give you a future and a hope. Then you will call upon Me and go and pray to Me, and I will listen to you.

Jeremiah 29:11-12 NKJV

In case you've been wondering, wonder no more—God does answer your prayers. What God does not do is this: He does not always answer your prayers as soon as you might like, and He does not always answer your prayers by saying "Yes."

God answers prayers not only according to our wishes but also according to His master plan. And guess what? We don't know that plan . . . but we can know the Planner.

Are you praying? Then you can be sure that God is listening. And sometime soon, He'll answer!

TODAY'S PRAYER

Dear Lord, You always hear my prayers. Remind me to pray often about the things I need and the things You want me to have. Amen

DAY 109

RESPECT FOR OTHERS

Being respected is more important than having great riches.

Proverbs 22:1 ICB

Do you try to have a respectful attitude towards everybody? Hopefully so!

Should you be respectful of grown ups? Of course. Teachers? Certainly. Family members? Yes. Friends? Yep, but it doesn't stop there. The Bible teaches us to treat all people with respect.

Respect for others is habit-forming: the more you do it, the easier it becomes. So start practicing right now. Say lots of kind words and do lots of kind things, because when it comes to kindness and respect, practice makes perfect.

TODAY'S PRAYER

Dear Lord, I will try to show respect to everybody, starting with my family and my friends. And, I will do my best to share the love that I feel in my heart for them . . . and for You! Amen

DAY 110

FORGIVE AS QUICKLY AS YOU CAN

Be gentle with one another, sensitive. Forgive one another as quickly and thoroughly as God in Christ forgave you.

Ephesians 4:32 MSG

How hard is it to forgive people? Sometimes, it's very hard! But God tells us that we must forgive other people, even when we'd rather not forgive them. So, if you're angry with anybody (or if you're upset by something you yourself have done), it's time to forgive.

God instructs us to treat other people exactly as we wish to be treated. When we forgive others, we are obeying our Heavenly Father, and that's exactly what we must try to do.

TODAY'S PRAYER

Dear Lord, I will forgive others. When I forgive other people, I know that I am obeying Your instructions. And I know that I am also getting rid of angry feelings that can hurt me more than they hurt anybody else. So, I will forgive and keep forgiving, just like You always forgive me. Amen

DAY 111

Real Friends

A friend loves you all the time.

Proverbs 17:17 ICB

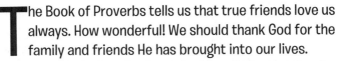

The Book of Proverbs tells us that true friends love us always. How wonderful! We should thank God for the family and friends He has brought into our lives.

Today, let's give thanks to God for all the people who love us, for brothers and sisters, parents and grandparents, aunts and uncles, cousins and friends. And then, as a way of thanking God, let's obey Him by being especially kind to our loved ones. They deserve it, and so does He.

A VERY VEGGIE BRIGHT IDEA

A true friend is a gift of God.

Robert South

TODAY'S PRAYER

Dear Lord, I thank You for my friends. And I thank You for my best friend: Jesus. Please let my love for Your Son be shown in the way I treat my friends. Amen

THE WORDS YOU SPEAK

If anyone considers himself religious and yet does not keep a tight rein on his tongue, he deceives himself and his religion is worthless.

James 1:26 NIV

The words you speak are important. If you speak kind words, you make other people feel better. And that's exactly what you should do!

How hard is it to say a kind word? Not very! Yet sometimes we're so busy that we forget to say the very things that might make other people feel better.

Kind words help; cruel words hurt. It's as simple as that. And, when we say the right thing at the right time, we give a gift that can change somebody's day or somebody's life.

TODAY'S PRAYER

Dear Lord, I know that You hear every word I say. Every day, I will try my best to say things that are honest, kind, and worthy of You. Amen

DAY 113

TRY TO MEMORIZE THIS VERSE

*For the Lord is good;
His mercy is everlasting,
and His truth endures
to all generations.*

Psalm 100:5 NKJV

*This is an important Bible verse. Practice saying it
several times. And then, talk to your mom or dad
about exactly what the verse means . . .*

A TIP FOR PARENTS
Today, talk to your child about . . . God's blessings.

TODAY'S PRAYER
Dear Lord, I have more blessings than I can
possibly count. Today, let me share Your
blessings with others, just as You first shared
them with me. Amen

DAY 114

everlasting Protection

The Lord is my rock, my fortress, and my deliverer, my God, my mountain where I seek refuge. My shield, the horn of my salvation, my stronghold, my refuge, and my Savior.

2 Samuel 22:2-3 HCSB

Life isn't always easy. Far from it! Sometimes, life can be very hard indeed. But even when we're upset or hurt, we must remember that we're protected by a loving Heavenly Father.

When we're worried, God can reassure us; when we're sad, God can comfort us. When our feelings are hurt, God is not just near, He is here. We must lift our thoughts and prayers to our Father in heaven. When we do, He will answer our prayers. Why? Because He is our Shepherd, and He has promised to protect us now and forever.

A TIP TO START YOUR DAY

The best protection comes from the loving heart of God–and from the salvation that flows from His only begotten Son.

TODAY'S PRAYER

Dear Lord, You watch over me now and forever. I thank You, Father, for Your love, for Your protection, and for Your Son. Amen

DAY 115

No More Tantrums

A patient person [shows] great understanding, but a quick-tempered one promotes foolishness.

Proverbs 14:29 HCSB

Temper tantrums are silly. And so is pouting. So, of course, is whining. When we lose our tempers, we say things that we shouldn't say, and we do things that we shouldn't do. Too bad!

The Bible tells us that it is foolish to become angry and that it is wise to remain calm. That's why we should learn to control our tempers before our tempers take control of us.

A TIP TO START YOUR DAY

If you think you're about to throw a tantrum, slow down, catch your breath, and walk away if you must. It's better to walk away–and keep walking–than it is to blurt out angry words that can't be un-blurted.

TODAY'S PRAYER

Dear Lord, help me to keep away from angry thoughts and angry people. And if I am tempted to have a temper tantrum, help me to calm down before I do. Amen

DAY 116

iT'S UP TO YOU!

The one who plants and the one who waters have the same purpose, and each will be rewarded for his own work.

1 Corinthians 3:8 NCV

D o want to be the kind of Christian that God intends for you to be? It's up to you! You'll be the one who will decide how you behave.

If you decide to obey God and trust His Son, you will be rewarded now and forever. So guard your heart and trust your Heavenly Father. He will never lead you astray.

A TIP TO START YOUR DAY

It's easy to blame others when you get into trouble . . . but it's wrong. Instead of trying to blame other people for your own misbehavior, take responsibility . . . and learn from your mistakes!

TODAY'S PRAYER

Dear Lord, thank You for watching over me. Help me understand what's right and do what's right, now and always. Amen

DAY 117

Love Yourself, Too!

God began doing a good work in you, and I am sure he will continue it until it is finished when Jesus Christ comes again.

Philippians 1:6 NCV

The Bible teaches you this lesson: you should love everybody–and the word "everybody" includes yourself. Do you treat yourself with honor and respect? You should. After all, God created you in a very special way, and He loves you very much. And if God thinks you are amazing and wonderful, shouldn't you think about yourself in the same way? Of course you should!

So remember this: God wants you to love everybody, including the person you see when you look in the mirror. And one more thing: when you learn how to respect the person in the mirror, you'll be better at respecting other people, too.

TODAY'S PRAYER

Dear Lord, help me be kind to everybody, including myself. And when I make a mistake, help me to forgive myself, just like I forgive other people when they make mistakes. Amen

DAY 118

The Master Teacher

This man came to Him at night and said, "Rabbi, we know that You have come from God as a teacher, for no one could perform these signs You do unless God were with him."

John 3:2 HCSB

Who was the greatest teacher in the history of the world? Jesus was . . and He still is! Jesus teaches us how to live, how to behave, and how to worship. Now, it's up to each of us, as Christians, to learn the important lessons that Jesus can teach.

Someday soon, you will have learned everything that Jesus has to teach you, right? WRONG!!!! Jesus will keep teaching you important lessons throughout your life. And that's good, because all of us, kids and grown-ups alike, have lots to learn . . . especially from the Master . . . and the Master, of course, is Jesus.

TODAY'S PRAYER

Dear Lord, I thank You for Jesus, the best friend this world has ever had. Jesus is my Friend and Savior. I will try to know Him better now and always. Amen

DAY 119

IT'S IMPORTANT TO BE KIND

I tell you the truth, anything you did for even the least of my people here, you also did for me.

Matthew 25:40 NCV

The Bible promises that if you're a nice person, good things will happen to you. That's one reason (but not the only reason) that it's important to be kind.

Do you listen to your heart when it tells you to be kind to other people? Hopefully, you do. After all, lots of people in the world aren't as fortunate as you are—and some of these folks are living very near you.

Ask your parents to help you find ways to do nice things for other people. And don't forget that everybody needs love, kindness, and respect, so you should always be ready to share those things, too.

TODAY'S PRAYER

Dear Lord, it's always the right time to be kind. Help me be kind every day of my life. Amen

DAY 120

TRY TO MEMORIZE THIS VERSE

*Guard your heart above all else,
for it is the source of life.*

Proverbs 4:23 HCSB

*This is an important Bible verse. Practice saying it
several times. And then, talk to your mom or dad
about exactly what the verse means . . .*

A TIP FOR PARENTS
Today, talk to your child about . . .
the need for all of us to guard our hearts.

TODAY'S PRAYER
Dear Lord, today I will guard my heart against
bad things and bad thoughts. All day long, I will
remember Your love, Your blessings, and Your Son.
Amen

The More You Share, The Better You'll Feel

He that giveth, let him do it with simplicity . . .

Romans 12:8 KJV

If you're having a little trouble learning how to share your stuff, you're not alone! Most people have problems letting go of the things they own, so don't be discouraged. Just remember that learning to share requires practice and lots of it. The more you share–and the more you learn how good it feels to share–the sooner you'll be able to please God with the generosity and love that flows from your heart.

TODAY'S PRAYER

Dear Lord, there are so many things that I can share. Help me never to forget the importance of sharing my possessions, my prayers, and my love with family members and friends. Amen

DAY 122

OBEYING THE GOLDEN RULE

So don't get tired of doing what is good. Don't get discouraged and give up, for we will reap a harvest of blessing at the appropriate time.

Galatians 6:9 NLT

The Bible teaches us to treat other people with respect, kindness, courtesy, and love. When we do, we make other people happy, we make God happy, and we feel better about ourselves, too.

So if you're wondering how to make the world—and your world—a better place, here's a great place to start: let the Golden Rule be your rule. When you do, you'll like yourself a little better . . . and so will other people.

A TIP TO START YOUR DAY

Use your head to handle yourself and your heart to handle others.

TODAY'S PRAYER

Dear Lord, when I am kind to other people, I feel better about myself. And, Your Bible teaches me about the Golden Rule. So help me obey the Golden Rule, Father, now and forever. Amen

DAY 123

VERY BIG IDEAS ABOUT TOO MUCH STUFF

To start your day, take a few minutes to talk to your mom or dad about what these two quotations mean.

There is absolutely no evidence that complexity and materialism lead to happiness. On the contrary, there is plenty of evidence that simplicity and spirituality lead to joy, a blessedness that is better than happiness.

Dennis Swanberg

If you want to be truly happy, you won't find it on an endless quest for more stuff. You'll find it in receiving God's generosity and then passing that generosity along.

Bill Hybels

TODAY'S PRAYER

Dear Lord, stuff isn't as important as some people think. Help me remember that the things I own aren't as important as the person I am becoming. Amen

DAY 124

Very Big Ideas About God's Protection

To start your day, take a few minutes to talk to your mom or dad about what these two quotations mean.

Under heaven's lock and key, we are protected by the most efficient security system available: the power of God.

Charles Swindoll

Prayer is our pathway not only to divine protection, but also to a personal, intimate relationship with God.

Shirley Dobson

TODAY'S PRAYER

Dear Lord, You watch over me now and forever. I thank You, Father, for Your love, for Your protection, and for Your Son. Amen

GOD IS ALWAYS WITH YOU

Fear not, for I am with you; be not dismayed, for I am your God. I will strengthen you.

Isaiah 41:10 NKJV

Here's a promise you can depend on: wherever you are, God is always there, too.

God doesn't take vacations, and He doesn't play hide-and-seek. He's always "right here, right now," waiting to hear from you. So if you're wondering where God is, wonder no more. He's here. And that's a promise!

A TIP TO START YOUR DAY

God's presence provides comfort. Seek Him often and pray often.

TODAY'S PRAYER

Dear Lord, You are always with me and You are always listening to my thoughts and to my prayers. I will pray to You often, and I will trust in You always. Amen

DAY 126

FOR GOD SO LOVED THE WORLD

For God so loved the world that he gave his only Son, so that everyone who believes in him will not perish but have eternal life.

John 3:16 NLT

I f God had a refrigerator in heaven, your picture would be on it! And that fact should make you feel very good about the person you are and the person you can become.

God's love for you is bigger and more wonderful than you can imagine. So do this, and do it right now: accept God's love with open arms and welcome His Son, Jesus, into your heart. When you do, you'll feel better about yourself . . . and your life will be changed forever.

TODAY'S PRAYER

Dear Lord, I thank You for loving me. And I thank You for sending Your Son Jesus to this earth so that I can receive Your gift of eternal love and eternal life. I will praise You, Dear God, today, tomorrow, and forever. Amen

DAY 127

GOD IS EVERYWHERE

God did this so that men would seek him and perhaps reach out for him and find him, though he is not far from each one of us.

Acts 17:27 NIV

God is everywhere you have ever been. And He is everywhere you will ever go. That's why you can speak to God any time you need to.

If you are afraid or discouraged, you can turn to God for strength. If you are worried, you can trust God's promises. And if you are happy, you can thank Him for His gifts.

God is right here, and so are you. And He's waiting patiently to hear from you, so why not have a word with Him right now?

A VERY VEGGIE BRIGHT IDEA

God is in the midst of whatever has happened, is happening, and will happen.

Charles Swindoll

TODAY'S PRAYER

Dear Lord, You never leave me, and You are always listening to my thoughts and to my prayers. Thank You, Father, for Your blessings and Your love. Amen

DAY 128

Be Quick to Share

And God will generously provide all you need. Then you will always have everything you need and plenty left over to share with others.

2 Corinthians 9:8 NLT

The Bible teaches that it's better to be generous than selfish. But sometimes, you won't feel like sharing your things, and you'll be tempted to keep everything for yourself. When you're feeling a little bit stingy, remember this: God wants you to share your things, and He will reward you when you do so.

When you learn to be a more generous person, God will be pleased with you . . . and you'll be pleased with yourself. So do yourself (and everybody else) a favor: be a little more generous, starting NOW!

TODAY'S PRAYER

Dear Lord, Jesus was never selfish. Let me follow in His footsteps by sharing with those who need my help. Amen

VERY BIG IDEAS ABOUT THE THINGS YOU SEE ON TV

To start your day, take a few minutes to talk to your mom or dad about what these two quotations mean.

Television has a way of attacking your senses and your heart. So be careful what you watch.

Criswell Freeman

If you give the devil an inch, he'll be a ruler.

Anonymous

TODAY'S PRAYER

Dear Lord, I know that many things on television are not good for me. Help me stay away from things that might hurt my heart. Amen

LOOK FOR THE GOOD IN OTHERS, AND THE GOOD IN YOURSELF

Dear friend, do not imitate what is evil, but what is good. The one who does good is of God; the one who does evil has not seen God.

3 John 1:11 HCSB

If you look for the good in other people, you'll probably find it. And, if you look for the good things in life, you'll probably find them, too.

But if you spend your time looking for things that aren't so good, you'll most certainly find plenty of bad things to look at. So what should you do? It's simple: you should look for the good things, of course.

When you start looking for good things, you'll find them everywhere: in church, at school, in your neighborhood, and at home.

So don't waste your time on things that make you feel angry, discouraged, worried, guilty, or afraid. Look, instead, for the good things in life, the things that God wants you to pay attention to. You'll be glad you did . . . and God will be glad, too.

TODAY'S PRAYER

Dear Lord, help me think good thoughts and look for the best in other people, now and forever. Amen

DAY 131

WHaT YouR Conscience Says aBouT ForGiveness

Now the goal of our instruction is love from a pure heart, a good conscience, and a sincere faith.

1 Timothy 1:5 HCSB

God gave you something called a conscience: it's that little feeling that tells you whether something is right or wrong. Your conscience will usually tell you what to do and when to do it. Trust that feeling.

If you listen to your conscience, it won't be as hard for you to forgive people. Why? Because forgiving other people is the right thing to do. And, it's what God wants you to do. And it's what your conscience tells you to do. So what are you waiting for?

TODAY'S PRAYER

Dear Lord, in my heart, I know that I should forgive other people. So when my heart tells me to forgive, that's exactly what I'll do. Amen

DAY 132

Peace at Home

My dear brothers, always be willing to listen and slow to speak. Do not become angry easily. Anger will not help you live a good life as God wants.

James 1:19 ICB

Sometimes, it's easy to become angry with family members, and sometimes it's hard to forgive them. After all, we know that our family will still love us no matter how angry we become. But while it's easy to become angry at home, it's usually wrong.

The next time you're tempted to stay angry at a brother, or a sister, or a parent, remember that these are the people who love you more than anybody else! Then, calm down, and forgive them . . . NOW! Because peace is always beautiful, especially when it's peace at your house.

TODAY'S PRAYER

Dear Lord, if I become angry with family or friends, calm me down. Help me learn to control my temper and to control myself. Jesus forgave everybody, even the people who hurt Him. I should, too. Amen

Make Everybody Proud

Give generously, for your gifts will return to you later.

Ecclesiastes 11:1 NLT

I t's tempting to be selfish, but it's wrong. It's tempting to want to keep everything for yourself, but it's better to share. It's tempting to say, "No, that's MINE!" but it's better to say, "I'll share it with you."

Are you sometimes tempted to be a little stingy? Are you sometimes tempted to say, "No, I don't want to share that!"—and then do you feel a little sorry that you said it? If that describes you, don't worry: everybody is tempted to be a little bit selfish. Your job is to remember this: even when it's tempting to be selfish, you should try very hard not to be. Because when you're generous, not selfish, you'll make your parents proud and you'll make your Father in heaven proud, too.

TODAY'S PRAYER

Dear Lord, the Bible teaches me that it is better to give than to receive. So, Father, help me be generous, kind, helpful, and grateful. Amen

DAY 134

Jesus is The Best Friend You'll ever Have

Greater love has no one than this, that he lay down his life for his friends.

John 15:13 NIV

There's an old song that says, "What a friend we have in Jesus." Those words are certainly true! When you invite Him into your heart, Jesus will be your friend today, tomorrow, and forever.

Jesus wants you to have a happy, healthy life. He wants you to behave yourself, and He wants you to take care of yourself. And now, it's up to you to do your best to live up to the hopes and dreams of your very best friend: Jesus.

A TIP TO START YOUR DAY

Of course you know that Jesus loves you. But it's up to you to make sure that your friends know it, too. So remind them often.

TODAY'S PRAYER

Dear Lord, thank You for Jesus, the light of my life. Amen

DAY 135

You're Not Expected to Be Perfect

If we confess our sins to him, he is faithful and just to forgive us and to cleanse us from every wrong.

1 John 1:9 NLT

When you make a mistake, do you get really mad at yourself . . . or maybe really, really, really mad? Hopefully not! After all, everybody makes mistakes, and nobody is expected to be perfect.

Even when you make mistakes, God loves you . . . so you should love yourself, too.

So the next time you make a mistake, learn from it. And after you've learned your lesson, try never to make that same mistake again. But don't be too hard on yourself. God doesn't expect you to be perfect, and since He loves you anyway, you should feel that way, too.

TODAY'S PRAYER

Dear Lord, when I make mistakes, I will admit what I've done, and I will apologize to the people I've hurt. You are perfect, Lord; I am not. I thank You for Your forgiveness and for Your love. Amen

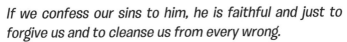

DAY 136

When People Are Not Nice

A kind man benefits himself, but a cruel man brings disaster on himself.

Proverbs 11:17 HCSB

ace it: sometimes people can be cruel. And when people are unkind to you or to your friends, you may be tempted to strike back in anger. Don't do it! Instead, remember that God corrects other people's behaviors in His own way, and He doesn't need your help. So even when other people misbehave, God wants you to forgive them . . . and that's what you should do.

A TIP TO START YOUR DAY

Do you know children who say or do cruel things to other kids? If so, don't join in! Instead, stand up for those who need your help. It's the right thing to do.

TODAY'S PRAYER

Dear Lord, some people can be cruel, but I know that I should never be cruel. Even if my friends behave badly, I want to do what's right, Lord. Help me do the right thing every day of my life. Amen

DAY 137

Friends Who Make You Better

My dear, dear friends, if God loved us like this, we certainly ought to love each other.

1 John 4:11 MSG

A re your friends the kind of kids who encourage you to behave yourself? If so, you've chosen your friends wisely.

But if your friends try to get you in trouble, perhaps it's time to think long and hard about making some new friends.

Whether you know it or not, you're probably going to behave like your friends behave. So pick out friends who make you want to behave better, not worse. When you do, you'll be saving yourself from a lot of trouble . . . a whole lot of trouble.

A TIP TO START YOUR DAY

Choose wise friends, and listen carefully to the things they say.

TODAY'S PRAYER

Dear Lord, the Bible teaches me to choose my friends carefully. And, that's what I intend to do every day of my life. Amen

DAY 138

Showing Others What it Means to Be a Christian

Do you want to be counted wise, to build a reputation for wisdom? Here's what you do: Live well, live wisely, live humbly. It's the way you live, not the way you talk, that counts.

James 3:13 MSG

How do people know that you're a Christian? Well, you can tell them, of course. And make no mistake about it: talking about your faith in God is a very good thing to do. But simply telling people about Jesus isn't enough. You must also be willing to show people how a real Christian (like you) should behave. Does that sound like a big responsibility? It is . . . but you can do it!

A TIP TO START YOUR DAY

The life you live is your most important testimony.

TODAY'S PRAYER

Dear Lord, I want You to use me as a good example for others to follow. So, I'll always do my best to follow in the footsteps of Your Son. Please let others see Him through me. Amen

DAY 139

Be Willing to Forgive

Talk and act like a person expecting to be judged by the Rule that sets us free. For if you refuse to act kindly, you can hardly expect to be treated kindly. Kind mercy wins over harsh judgment every time.

James 2:12-13 MSG

The Bible tells us this: when other people do things that are wrong, we should forgive them. God's Word also tells us that when we're willing to forgive others, God is quick to forgive us for the mistakes that we make.

Has somebody done something that makes you angry? Talk things over with your mom or dad, and then be ready to forgive the person who has hurt your feelings. And remember: God wants you to hurry up and forgive others, just like God is always in a hurry to forgive you.

TODAY'S PRAYER

Dear Lord, when I have trouble forgiving someone, when I'm discouraged, or tired, or angry, let me turn to You for strength, for patience, for wisdom, and for love. Amen

THE THINGS YOU OWN AREN'T AS IMPORTANT AS YOU MAY THINK

Don't be obsessed with getting more material things. Be relaxed with what you have.

Hebrews 13:5 MSG

Here's something to remember about stuff: it's not that important!

Lots of people are in love with money and the things that money can buy. God is not. God cares about people, not possessions, and so must you.

You should not be too concerned about the clothes you wear or the things you own. Your material possessions aren't nearly as important as the love that you feel in your heart–love for your family, love for your friends, and love for your Father in heaven.

TODAY'S PRAYER

Dear God, the Bible teaches me that the things I own aren't very important. So let me think more about the person I want to become and less about the things I want to own. Amen

DAY 141

GOD is WATCHING

Remember that those who do good prove that they are God's children, and those who do evil prove that they do not know God.

3 John 1:11 NLT

Even when nobody's watching, God is. And He knows whether you've done the right thing or the wrong thing. So if you're tempted to misbehave when nobody is looking, remember this: there is never a time when "nobody's watching." Somebody is always watching over you–and that Somebody, of course, is your Father in heaven. Don't let Him down!

A TIP TO START YOUR DAY

Remember, your actions speak much more loudly than your words . . . so behave accordingly.

TODAY'S PRAYER

Dear Lord, show me the right thing to do–and help me do it–today and every day of my life. Amen

DAY 142

GOOD AND EVIL

Friend, don't go along with evil. Model the good. The person who does good does God's work. The person who does evil falsifies God, doesn't know the first thing about God.

3 John 1:11 MSG

When other people are unkind, you may be tempted to strike back in anger. But God doesn't want you to fight your way through life! God wants you to forgive other people, even when they haven't behaved themselves, even when they've been very mean. So, when other people aren't nice, forgive them as quickly as you can. And let God take care of everything else.

A VERY VEGGIE BRIGHT IDEA

God shapes the world by prayer. The more praying there is in the world, the better the world will be, and the mightier will be the forces against evil.

E. M. Bounds

TODAY'S PRAYER

Dear Lord, when other people do bad things, I won't copy them, and I won't join them. I'll try my best to behave myself and stay far away from people who don't. Amen

DAY 143

Very Big ideas about Respecting Other People

To start your day, take a few minutes to talk to your mom or dad about what these two quotations mean.

Don't be a half-Christian. There are too many of them in the world already. The world has a profound respect for a person who is sincere in his faith.

Billy Graham

If you are willing to honor a person out of respect for God, you can be assured that God will honor you.

Beth Moore

TODAY'S PRAYER

Dear Lord, help me respect other people, and help me respect You. Let me be a respectful person so that other people can see what it means to be a Christian. Amen

DAY 144

Making The Right Choices

But Daniel purposed in his heart that he would not defile himself....

Daniel 1:8 KJV

Your life is a series of choices. From the instant you wake up in the morning until the moment you nod off to sleep at night, you make lots of decisions: decisions about the things you do, decisions about the words you speak, and decisions about the thoughts you choose to think.

So, if you want to lead a life that is pleasing to God, you must make choices that are pleasing to Him. He deserves no less . . . and neither, for that matter, do you.

A TIP TO START YOUR DAY

When you make wise choices, you make everybody happy.

TODAY'S PRAYER

Lord, help me make choices that are pleasing to You. Help me to be honest, patient, and kind. And, help me to follow the teachings of Jesus, not just today, but every day. Amen

DAY 145

TRY TO MEMORIZE THIS VERSE

*I have learned to be content
in whatever circumstances I am.*

Philippians 4:11 HCSB

*This is an important Bible verse. Practice saying it
several times. And then, talk to your mom or dad
about exactly what the verse means . . .*

A TIP FOR PARENTS
Today, talk to your child about . . .
finding true contentment

TODAY'S PRAYER
Dear Lord, You have given me so many
blessings, and I thank You. Today and every
day, I will be content with the things I have,
and I will share the things I have. Amen

DAY 146

LOVING PEOPLE WHO ARE HARD TO LOVE

You have heard it said, "Love your neighbor and hate your enemy." But I tell you: Love your enemies and pray for those who persecute you, that you may be sons of your Father in heaven.

Matthew 5:43-45 NIV

Sometimes people can be rude . . . very rude. As long as you live here on earth, you will face countless opportunities to lose your temper when other folks behave badly. But God has a better plan: He wants you to forgive people and move on. Remember that God has already forgiven you, so it's only right that you should be willing to forgive others.

So here's some good advice: forgive everybody as quickly as you can, and leave the rest up to God.

TODAY'S PRAYER

Heavenly Father, make me a kind person even to those who don't treat me kindly. Let me forgive others, just as You have forgiven me. Amen

Try to Memorize This Verse

*A gentle answer turns away wrath,
but a harsh word stirs up anger.*

Proverbs 15:1 NIV

*This is an important Bible verse. Practice saying it
several times. And then, talk to your mom or dad
about exactly what the verse means . . .*

A TIP FOR PARENTS
Today, talk to your child about . . .
the words they speak.

TODAY'S PRAYER
Dear Lord, if I choose my words carefully, I can
make everybody happier, including myself. Every day,
help me choose the words that You want me to speak
so that I can make my corner of the world a better place
to live. Amen

You Can't Buy Happiness

Since we entered the world penniless and will leave it penniless, if we have bread on the table and shoes on our feet, that's enough.

1 Timothy 6:7-8 MSG

ere's a question to think about today: How much stuff is too much stuff? Well, if your desire for stuff is getting in the way of your desire to know God, then you've got too much stuff–it's as simple as that.

If you find yourself worrying too much about stuff, it's time to change the way you think about the things you own. Stuff isn't really very important to God, and it shouldn't be too important to you.

TODAY'S PRAYER

Dear God, help me remember that the stuff I own isn't very important. What's really important is the love that I feel in my heart for my family, the love that I feel for Jesus, and the love that I feel for You. Amen

OBEDIENCE IS A CHOICE

*Those who obey his commands live in him, and he in them.
And this is how we know that he lives in us: We know it by
the Spirit he gave us.*

1 John 3:24 NIV

You have a choice to make: Are you going to be an obedient boy or not? And remember: the decision to be obedient–or the decision not to be obedient– is a decision that you must make for yourself.

If you decide to behave yourself, you've made a smart choice. If you decide to obey your parents, you've made another smart choice. If you decide to pay attention to your teachers, you've made yet another wise choice. BUT . . . if you decide not to be obedient, you've made a silly choice.

What kind of person will you choose to be? An obedient, well-behaved person or the opposite? Before you answer that question, here's something to think about: obedience pays . . . and disobedience doesn't.

TODAY'S PRAYER

Dear Lord, when I play by Your rules, You give me wonderful rewards. I will read the Bible, Lord, so I can learn Your rules–and I will obey Your rules, now and forever. Amen

DAY 150

Very Big ideas about God's Help

To start your day, take a few minutes to talk to your mom or dad about what these two quotations mean.

Things can be very difficult for us, but nothing is too hard for Him.
Charles Stanley

God never leads us astray. He knows exactly where He's taking us. Our job is to obey.
Charles Swindoll

TODAY'S PRAYER

Dear Lord, when I want to give up, help me remember how important it is to keep trying. And when I'm worried or upset, help me remember to talk to my parents and to You. Amen

DAY 151

Don't Get Lost in the Crowd

We must obey God rather than men.

Acts 5:29 HCSB

Rick Warren observed, "Those who follow the crowd usually get lost in it." We know those words to be true, but oftentimes we fail to live by them. Instead of trusting God for guidance, we imitate our friends and suffer the consequences.

Instead of getting lost in the crowd, you should find guidance from your parents and from God. When you do, you'll be happier . . . much happier!

A TIP TO START YOUR DAY

Being obedient to God means that you cannot always please other people.

TODAY'S PRAYER

Dear Lord, other people may want me to misbehave, but You want me to behave myself. And that's what I want, too–I want to do what's right. So help me do the right thing, Lord, even when it's hard. Amen

DAY 152

GET OVER IT

Do not remember the past events, pay no attention to things of old. Look, I am about to do something new; even now it is coming. Do you not see it? Indeed, I will make a way in the wilderness, rivers in the desert.

Isaiah 43:18-19 HCSB

An important part of learning how to forgive is learning how to get over the things that happened yesterday. What happened yesterday is past. And, if what happened yesterday has made you unhappy, today is as good a day as any to start getting over your hurt feelings.

Are you still angry with someone? Has that person said he was sorry and tried to make things better? If so, talk to your parents about it! They'll help you understand that you can't change the past, but you can get over it.

TODAY'S PRAYER

Dear Lord, let me learn from what happened yesterday, but don't let me stay angry about what happened yesterday. Let me forgive others just as You have forgiven me, and let me be a happy, cheerful person today and every day. Amen

DAY 153

TRY TO MEMORIZE THIS VERSE

*Cast your burden on the Lord,
and He will support you;
He will never allow the righteous
to be shaken.*

Psalm 55:22 HCSB

This is an important Bible verse. Practice saying it several times. And then, talk to your mom or dad about exactly what the verse means . . .

A TIP FOR PARENTS

Today, talk to your child about . . .
God's strength.

TODAY'S PRAYER

Dear Lord, You are always with me, protecting me and encouraging me. Whatever this day may bring, I thank You for Your love and for Your strength. And I will trust You, Father, today and forever. Amen

DAY 154

Your Family Has Rules

This is how we are sure that we have come to know Him: by keeping His commands.

1 John 2:3 HCSB

Your family has rules . . . rules that you're not supposed to break.

If you're old enough to know right from wrong, then you're old enough to do something about it. In other words, you should always try to obey your family's rules.

How can you tell "the right thing" from "the wrong thing"? By listening carefully to your parents, that's how.

The more self-control you have, the easier it is to obey your parents. Why? Because, when you learn to think first and do things next, you avoid making silly mistakes. So here's what you should do: First, slow down long enough to listen to your parents. Then, do the things that you know your parents want you to do.

TODAY'S PRAYER

Dear Lord, when I obey Your rules, good things happen. One of Your rules is very simple: to obey my parents. So here's what I'm asking for, Lord: help me listen to my parents . . . and help me obey them. Amen

LISTENING QUIETLY AND CAREFULLY

A wise man will hear and increase in learning, and a man of understanding will acquire wise counsel.

Proverbs 1:5 NASB

Have you learned how to sit quietly and listen to your parents and to your teachers? Have you learned how to listen respectfully–with your ears open wide and your mouth closed tight? If so, give yourself a big pat on the back (or if you can't reach way back there, ask your mom or dad to do it for you!).

An important part of learning self-control is learning how to be quiet when you're supposed to be quiet. It isn't always easy, but the sooner you learn how to sit quietly and behave respectfully, the better. So you might as well start now.

TODAY'S PRAYER

Dear Lord, make me a good listener, especially when I'm listening to people who have much to teach me. Amen

DAY 156

Be Patient

Don't work hard only when your master is watching and then shirk when he isn't looking; work hard and with gladness all the time, as though working for Christ, doing the will of God with all your hearts.

Ephesians 6:6-7 TLB

If you've lost patience with someone, or if you're angry, take a deep breath and then ask yourself a simple question: "How would Jesus behave if He were here?" The answer to that question will tell you what to do.

Jesus was quick to speak kind words, and He was quick to forgive others. We must do our best to be like Him. When we do, we will be patient, loving, understanding, and kind.

A VERY VEGGIE BRIGHT IDEA

Patience achieves more than force.

Edmund Burke

TODAY'S PRAYER

Dear Lord, thank You for loving me and forgiving me. I will return Your love by sharing it . . . now and always. Amen

iT Pays To Praise

Is anyone happy? Let him sing songs of praise.

James 5:13 NIV

The Bible makes it clear: it pays to say "thank You" to God. But sometimes, we may not feel like thanking anybody, not even our Father in heaven.

If we ever stop praising God, it's a big mistake . . . a VERY BIG mistake.

When you stop to think about it, God has been very generous with you . . . and He deserves a great big "thanks" for all those amazing gifts.

Do you want an attitude that pleases God? Then make sure that your attitude praises God. And don't just praise Him on Sunday morning. Praise Him every day, starting with this one.

A TIP TO START YOUR DAY

When you pray, don't just ask God for things; also praise Him.

TODAY'S PRAYER

Heavenly Father, I am Yours. Use me to make this world a better place as I share the Good News of Your Son, today and every day. Amen

DAY 158

KEEP LEARNING ABOUT SELF-CONTROL

For the Son of man shall come in the glory of his Father with his angels; and then he shall reward every man according to his works.

Matthew 16:27 KJV

Who needs to learn more about self-control? You do! Why? Well, for one thing, you'll discover that good things happen to boys (like you) who are wise enough to think ahead and smart enough look before they leap.

Whether you're at home or at school, you'll learn that the best rewards go to the kids who control their behavior–not to the people who let their behaviors control them!

TODAY'S PRAYER

Dear Lord, as I grow up, I want to be able to control myself better and better each day. Let me learn the wisdom of looking before I leap. And let me make choices that are pleasing to You. Amen

THINK AHEAD AND LOOK AHEAD

Learn the truth and never reject it. Get wisdom, self-control, and understanding.

Proverbs 23:23 NCV

Maybe you've heard this old saying: "Look before you leap." What does that saying mean? It means that you should stop and think before you do something. Otherwise, you might be sorry you did it.

Your parents are trying to teach you how to slow down and make better decisions. Why? Because your parents want what's best for you, that's why!

So here's something that you can do: think about the consequences of your behaviors before you do something silly . . . or dangerous . . . or both.

A TIP TO START YOUR DAY

When you learn how to control yourself, you'll be happier . . . and your parents will be happier, too.

TODAY'S PRAYER

Dear Lord, I want to be able to control myself better and better each day. Help me find better ways to behave myself in ways that are pleasing to You. Amen

each Day is a Gift

How happy are those who can live in your house, always singing your praises. How happy are those who are strong in the Lord . . .

Psalm 84:4-5 NLT

God wants you to have a happy, joyful life. But that doesn't mean that you'll be happy all the time. Sometimes, you won't feel like feeling happy, and when you don't, your attitude won't be very good.

When you're feeling a little tired or sad, here's something to remember: this day is a gift from God. And it's up to you to enjoy this day by trying to be cheerful, helpful, courteous, and well behaved. How can you do these things? A good place to start is by doing your best to think good thoughts.

TODAY'S PRAYER

Dear Lord, I have more blessings than I can count. Now and always, I will be a happy Christian as I give thanks for Your gifts and for Your Son. Amen

a Royal Law

This royal law is found in the Scriptures: "Love your neighbor as yourself." If you obey this law, then you are doing right.

James 2:8 ICB

James was the brother of Jesus and a leader of the early Christian church. In a letter that is now a part of the New Testament, James reminded his friends of a "royal law." That law is the Golden Rule.

When we treat others in the same way that we wish to be treated, we are doing the right thing. James knew it, and so, of course, did his brother Jesus. Now we should learn the same lesson: it's nice to be nice; it's good to be good; and it's great to be kind.

TODAY'S PRAYER

Dear Lord, the Bible teaches me how to treat other people–I should treat them like I want to be treated. So, I'll try hard to obey Your Golden Rule now and forever. Amen

DAY 162

LETTING CHRIST'S JOY BECOME YOUR JOY

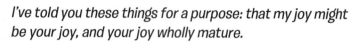

I've told you these things for a purpose: that my joy might be your joy, and your joy wholly mature.

John 15:11 MSG

Christ made it clear to His followers: He intended that His joy would become their joy. And it's still true today: Christ intends that His believers share His love with His joy in their hearts. Yet sometimes, amid the inevitable hustle and bustle of life, we can lose—at least for a while—the joy of Christ as we wrestle with the challenges of daily living.

C. H. Spurgeon, the 19th-century English clergyman, advised, "The Lord is glad to open the gate to every knocking soul. It opens very freely. Have faith and enter at this moment through holy courage. If you knock with a heavy heart, you shall yet sing with joy of spirit. Never be discouraged!" How true!

TODAY'S PRAYER

Dear Lord, help me to feel Your joy—and help me to share it—today, tomorrow, and every day. Amen

DAY 163

iT FeeLs GooD To OBeY anD ForGive

This is love for God: to obey his commands.

1 John 5:3 NIV

We know that it's right to forgive other people and wrong to stay angry with them. But sometimes, it's so much easier to do the wrong thing than it is to do the right thing, especially when we're tired or frustrated.

When you do the right thing by forgiving other people, you'll feel good because you'll know that you're obeying God. And that's a very good feeling indeed. So make this promise to yourself and keep it: play by the rules–God's rules. You'll always be glad you did.

A TIP TO START YOUR DAY

Your obedience to God is a way to show Him that you're thankful for the blessings He has given you.

TODAY'S PRAYER

Dear Lord, You know what's best for me. I will study Your Word and obey Your teachings this day and forever. Amen

DAY 164

THE BEST TIME TO SHARE

Never walk away from someone who deserves help; your hand is God's hand for that person.

Proverbs 3:27 MSG

When is the best time to share? Whenever you can—and that means right now, if possible. When you start thinking about the things you can share, you probably think mostly about things that belong to you (like toys or clothes), but there are many other things you can share (like love, kindness, encouragement, and prayers). That means you have the opportunity to share something with somebody almost any time you want. And that's exactly what God wants you to do—so start sharing now, and don't ever stop.

A VERY VEGGIE BRIGHT IDEA

It is the duty of every Christian to be Christ to his neighbor.

Martin Luther

TODAY'S PRAYER

Dear Lord, help me to be a kind and generous person. The Bible tells me to share my things. I won't wait to share them; I will share them now. Amen

DAY 165

Very Big ideas about Perfectionism

To start your day, take a few minutes to talk to your mom or dad about what these two quotations mean.

The happiest people in the world
are not those who have no problems,
but the people who have learned
to live with those things
that are less than perfect.

James Dobson

What makes a Christian a Christian
is not perfection but forgiveness.

Max Lucado

TODAY'S PRAYER

Dear Lord, help me remember that I don't
have to be perfect to be wonderful. Amen

DAY 166

You're Special

Blessed is the man who does not condemn himself.

Romans 14:22 HCSB

When God made you, He made you in a very special way. In fact, you're a wonderful, one-of-a-kind creation, a special person unlike any other.

Do you realize how special you are? Do you know that God loves you because of who you are (not because of the things you've done)? And do you know that God has important things for you to do? Well, whether you realize it or not, all these things are all true.

So the next time you feel bad about something you've done, take a look in the mirror, and remember that you're looking at a wonderfully special person . . . you!

God loves you; your parents love you; your family loves you . . . and that's the way that you should feel about yourself, too.

TODAY'S PRAYER

Dear Lord, thank You for making me a special person. I am Your child, Father. So I will celebrate the person I am today. And I will celebrate the person I hope to become tomorrow. Amen

God's Love for You is Real

You are my God, and I will give you thanks; you are my God, and I will exalt you. Give thanks to the LORD, for he is good; his love endures forever.

Psalm 118:28-29 NIV

God's love is real, and it's meant for you. In fact, God loves you so much that He sent His only begotten Son so that you can join Jesus forever in heaven.

Today, remember that the best way to say "thank You" to God is to obey His commandments, to honor His Son, and to be kind to everybody.

A VERY VEGGIE BRIGHT IDEA

The love of God is one of the great realities of the universe.

A. W. Tozer

TODAY'S PRAYER

Dear Lord, today and every day, I thank You for Your Son, Jesus, and for His love. You sent Your Son to this earth so that I can live with Him forever in heaven. I praise You, Father, for this incredible gift. Amen

DAY 168

Keep Growing Up

Therefore, leaving the elementary message about the Messiah, let us go on to maturity.

Hebrews 6:1 HCSB

When will you be completely grown up? Hopefully never! God has a way of helping you continue to grow as a Christian throughout your entire life if you continue to worship Him.

If you learn about God's Word and talk to Him through your prayers, He has much to teach you, so keep learning about your Heavenly Father. And never stop.

A VERY VEGGIE BRIGHT IDEA

The strength of our spiritual lives will be in exact proportion to the place held by the Bible in our lives and in our thoughts.

George Mueller

TODAY'S PRAYER

Dear Lord, You have given me so many blessings, and I thank You. I will be content with the things I have, and I will share the things I have. Amen

You Have So Much To Be Thankful For!

And whatever you do, in word or in deed, do everything in the name of the Lord Jesus, giving thanks to God the Father through Him.

Colossians 3:17 HCSB

D o you have a thankful attitude? Hopefully so! After all, you've got plenty of things to be thankful for. Even during those times when you're angry or tired, you're a very lucky person.

Who has given you all the blessings you enjoy? Your parents are responsible, of course. But all of your blessings really start with God. That's why you should say "thank You" to God many times each day. He's given you so much . . . so thank Him, starting now.

TODAY'S PRAYER

Lord, You have plans for my life that are better than I can imagine. I will trust You to take care of my future, and I will try my best to obey Your rules, now and always. Amen

iT's impoRtanT to TeLL THe TRUTH

He has showed you, O man, what is good. And what does the LORD require of you? To act justly and to love mercy and to walk humbly with your God.

Micah 6:8 NIV

If you're tempted to say something that isn't true, stop and ask yourself a simple question: "How would Jesus behave if He were here?" The answer to that question will tell you what to say.

Jesus told His followers that the truth would make them free. As believers, we must do our best to know the truth and to tell it. When we do, we behave as our Savior behaved, and that's exactly how God wants us to behave.

TODAY'S PRAYER

Dear Lord, let me use Jesus as my example for living. When I have questions about what to do or how to act, let me behave as He behaved. When I do so, I will be patient, loving, and kind, not just today, but every day. Amen

DAY 171

Always Count Your Blessings

Enter his gates with thanksgiving; go into his courts with praise. Give thanks to him and bless his name. For the Lord is good. His unfailing love continues forever, and his faithfulness continues to each generation.

Psalm 100:4-5 NLT

If you sat down and began counting your blessings, how long would it take? A very, very long time! Your blessings include your life, your family, your friends, your talents, and your possessions, for starters. But, your greatest blessing–a gift that is yours for the asking–is God's gift of eternal life through Christ Jesus.

You can never count up every single blessing that God has given you, but it doesn't hurt to try . . . so get ready, get set, go–start counting your blessings RIGHT NOW!

TODAY'S PRAYER

Dear Lord, You have given me so many gifts, and I am so very grateful for all those blessings. Let me use my gifts, Lord, and let me help my friends use theirs. Amen

DAY 172

every Day is a Special Day

David and the whole house of Israel were celebrating before the Lord.

2 Samuel 6:5 HCSB

Every day should be a time for celebration, and hopefully, you feel like celebrating! After all, this day (like every other day) gives you the chance to thank God for all the wonderful things He has given you.

So don't wait for birthdays or holidays—make every day a special day, including this one. Take time to pause and thank God for His gifts. He deserves your thanks, and you deserve to celebrate!

A VERY VEGGIE BRIGHT IDEA

May your day be fashioned with joy, sprinkled with dreams, and touched by the miracle of love.

Barbara Johnson

TODAY'S PRAYER

Dear Lord, because of Your blessings, I can be joyful now and forever. So I will be a happy Christian, quick to smile and slow to frown. Amen

DAY 173

THAT LITTLE VOICE

For God is pleased with you when, for the sake of your conscience, you patiently endure unfair treatment.

1 Peter 2:19 NLT

When you know that you're doing what's right, you'll feel better about yourself. Why? Because you have a little voice in your head called your "conscience." Your conscience is a feeling that tells you whether something is right or wrong—and it's a feeling that makes you feel better about yourself when you know you've done the right thing.

Your conscience is an important tool. Pay attention to it!

The more you listen to your conscience, the easier it is to behave yourself. So here's great advice: first, slow down long enough to figure out the right thing to do—and then do it! When you do, you'll be proud of yourself . . . and other people will be proud of you, too.

TODAY'S PRAYER

Dear Lord, You have given me a conscience that tells me what is right and what is wrong. I will listen to that quiet voice so I can do the right thing every day of my life. Amen

STOP AND THINK

Now you must rid yourselves of all such things as these: anger, rage, malice . . .

Colossians 3:8 NIV

When we lose control of our emotions, we do things that we shouldn't do. Sometimes, we throw tantrums. How silly! Other times we pout or whine. Too bad!

The Bible tells us that it is foolish to become angry and that it is wise to remain calm. That's why we should learn to slow down and think about things before we do them.

Do you want to make life better for yourself and for your family? Then be patient and think things through. Stop and think before you do things, not after. It's the wise thing to do.

TODAY'S PRAYER

Dear Lord, You know that I can be impatient at times. And sometimes, I lose my temper. When I become upset, calm me down, Lord, and help me forgive the people who have made me angry. I know that Jesus forgave other people, and I should, too. Amen

Read Your Bible Every Day!

For I am not ashamed of the gospel, because it is God's power for salvation to everyone who believes.

Romans 1:16 HCSB

If you want to know God, you should read the book He wrote. It's called the Bible (of course!), and God uses it to teach you and guide you. The Bible is not like any other book. It is an amazing gift from your Heavenly Father.

D. L. Moody observed, "The Bible was not given to increase our knowledge but to change our lives." God's Holy Word is, indeed, a life-changing, one-of-a-kind treasure. Handle it with care, but more importantly, handle it every day!

TODAY'S PRAYER

Dear Lord, I thank You for Your Bible. It is a priceless gift to me, to my family, and to the world. I will use Your Word to learn how to think, how to pray, and how to behave. Amen

SHARING THE GOOD NEWS

But respect Christ as the holy Lord in your hearts. Always be ready to answer everyone who asks you to explain about the hope you have.

1 Peter 3:15 NCV

Every Christian, each in his or her own way, has a responsibility to share the Good News of our Jesus. And it's important to remember that we bear testimony through both words and actions. Wise Christians follow the advice of St. Francis of Assisi who advised, "Preach the gospel at all times and, if necessary, use words."

As you think about how your example influences others, remember that actions speak louder than words . . . much louder!

TODAY'S PRAYER

Dear Lord, I am only here on this earth for a while. But, because of Your Son, Jesus, I will be with You forever in heaven. Let me share that Good News with my family and friends. Amen

THE TRUTH WILL MAKE YOU FREE

Go after a life of love as if your life depended on it—because it does. Give yourselves to the gifts God gives you. Most of all, try to proclaim his truth.

1 Corinthians 14:1 MSG

Jesus had a message for his followers. He said, "The truth will set you free" (John 8:32 NIV). When we do the right thing and tell the truth, we don't need to worry about our lies catching up with us. When we behave honestly, we don't have to worry about feeling guilty or ashamed. But, if we fail to do what we know is right, bad things start to happen, and we feel guilty.

Jesus understood that the truth is a very good thing indeed. We should understand it, too. And we should keep telling it as long as we live.

TODAY'S PRAYER

Dear Lord, help me tell the truth, even when it's hard. Amen

DAY 178

WHAT TO DO WHEN
YOU'RE WORRIED

Give all your worries and cares to God, for he cares about what happens to you.

1 Peter 5:6 NLT

When we're worried, there are two places we should take our concerns: to the people who love and care for us and to God.

When troubles arise, it helps to talk about them with parents, grandparents, and concerned adults.

But we shouldn't stop there: we should also talk to God through our prayers. If you're worried about something, you can pray about it any time you want. And remember that God is always listening, and He always wants to hear from you.

So when you're worried, try this plan: talk and pray. Talk to the grown-ups who love you, and pray to the Heavenly Father who made you. The more you talk and the more you pray, the better you'll feel.

TODAY'S PRAYER

Dear Lord, when I am worried, I know where to turn for help: to those who love me, and to You. Thank You for the people who love and care for me, and thank You, Lord, for Your love. Amen

DAY 179

Don't Whine!

*Words kill, words give life; they're either poison or fruit—
you choose.*

Proverbs 18:21 MSG

D o you like to listen to other children whine? No way!
And since you don't like to hear other kids whining,
then you certainly shouldn't whine, either.

Sometimes, kids think that whining is a good way to
get the things they want . . . but it's not! So if your parents
or your teacher ask you to do something, don't complain
about it. And if there's something you want, don't whine
and complain until you get it.

Remember: whining won't make you happy . . . and it
won't make anybody else happy, either.

A TIP TO START YOUR DAY

Whining makes you sad, and it makes other people sad,
too. So, don't whine!

TODAY'S PRAYER

Dear Lord, let me count my blessings and be
thankful. And help me remember not to whine
about the things I don't have. Amen

DAY 180

Be a Good Citizen and a Good Christian

Make the Master proud of you by being good citizens. Respect the authorities, whatever their level; they are God's emissaries for keeping order.

1 Peter 2:13-14 MSG

D o you behave differently because you're a Christian? Or do you behave in pretty much the same way that you would if you had never heard of Jesus? Hopefully, your behavior is better because of the things you've learned from the Bible.

Doing the right thing is not always easy, especially when you're tired or frustrated. But, doing the wrong thing almost always leads to trouble. So here's some advice: remember the lessons you learn from the Bible. And keep remembering them every day of your life.

TODAY'S PRAYER

Dear Lord, help me to slow down and to think about my behavior. And then, help me to do the right thing so that I can feel better about myself . . . and You can, too. Amen

DAY 181

WAITING YOUR TURN

Don't be impatient for the Lord to act! Travel steadily along his path. He will honor you. . . .

Psalm 37:34 NLT

When we're standing in line or waiting our turn, it's tempting to scream, "Me first!" It's tempting, but it's the wrong thing to do! The Bible tells us that we shouldn't push ahead of other people; instead, we should do the right thing–and the polite thing–by saying, "You first!"

Sometimes, waiting your turn can be hard, especially if you're excited or in a hurry. But even then, waiting patiently is the right thing to do. Why? Because parents say so, teachers say so, and, most importantly, God says so!

TODAY'S PRAYER

Dear Lord, when I'm waiting for other people, give me patience. So, Father, please help me remember to follow the Golden Rule and wait my turn.

DAY 182

TRY TO MEMORIZE THIS VERSE

Be still,
and know that I am God.

Psalm 46:10 NKJV

This is an important Bible verse.
Practice saying it several times.
And then, talk to your mom or dad about
exactly what the verse means . . .

A TIP FOR PARENTS

Today, talk to your child about . . . God's constant
presence and His constant love.

TODAY'S PRAYER

Dear Lord, You are always with us, and You are always
listening to our thoughts and to our prayers. We will pray
to You often, and we will trust in You always. Amen

FIGURING OUT WHAT'S REALLY IMPORTANT

A pretentious, showy life is an empty life; a plain and simple life is a full life.

Proverbs 13:7 MSG

The Bible teaches this important lesson: it's not good to be too concerned about money or the stuff that money can buy. So don't worry too much about the things you can buy in stores. Worry more about obeying your parents and obeying your Heavenly Father–that's what's really important.

A TIP TO START YOUR DAY

The world says, "Buy more stuff." God says, "Stuff isn't important." Believe God.

TODAY'S PRAYER

Dear Lord, the world says that the things I own are important, but You say that it's what is inside my heart that really matters. So, I will think more about the person I am becoming and less about the things I own. Amen

CHRIST OFFERS Peace

I have told you these things, so that in me you may have peace. In this world you will have trouble. But take heart! I have overcome the world.

John 16:33 NIV

Jesus offers us peace . . . peace in our hearts and peace in our homes. But He doesn't force us to enjoy His peace–we can either accept His peace or not.

When we accept the peace of Jesus Christ by opening up our hearts to Him, we feel much better about ourselves, our families, and our lives.

Would you like to feel a little better about yourself and a little better about your corner of the world? Then open up your heart to Jesus, because that's where real peace begins.

TODAY'S PRAYER

Dear Lord, I thank You for my family. Help me treat everybody in my family with love and respect, today, tomorrow, and every day. Amen

NOBODY'S PERFECT

For everything created by God is good, and nothing should be rejected if it is received with thanksgiving.

1 Timothy 4:4 HCSB

Face facts: nobody's perfect . . . not even you! And remember this: it's perfectly okay not to be perfect. In fact, God doesn't expect you to be perfect, and you shouldn't expect yourself to be perfect, either.

Are you one of those people who can't stand to make a mistake? Do you think that you must please everybody all the time? When you make a mess of things, do you become terribly upset? If so, here's some advice: DON'T BE SO HARD ON YOURSELF! Mistakes happen . . . and besides, if you learn something from your mistakes, you'll become a better person.

TODAY'S PRAYER

Dear Lord, I don't want to make mistakes, but when I make them, let me learn from them. And, then, let me forgive myself as quickly as I can. Amen

DAY 186

Since You're Responsible, Be Responsible

So then each of us shall give account of himself to God.

Romans 14:12 NKJV

I n the Book of Galatians, Paul writes, "We must not tire of doing good." And that's an important lesson: even when we're tired or frustrated, we must do our best to do the right thing.

So the next time you're tempted to lose your temper or to do something unwise, stop for a moment and think. And, while you're thinking, remember that you're the one who's responsible for your own behavior—so please don't get tired of doing what's right!

TODAY'S PRAYER

Dear Lord, there's a right way and a wrong way to do things. Let me do what's right and keep doing what's right every day of my life. Amen

DAY 187

TRY TO MEMORIZE THIS VERSE

God loves a cheerful giver.
2 Corinthians 9:7 HCSB

*This is an important Bible verse about sharing.
Practice saying it several times.
And then, talk to your mom or dad about exactly
what the verse means . . .*

A TIP FOR PARENTS
Today, talk to your child about . . . the joy of giving.

TODAY'S PRAYER
Lord, make me a generous and cheerful Christian. Let me be kind to the people who need my help, and let me share my things, now and forever. Amen

Self-Control and Patience

All athletes practice strict self-control. They do it to win a prize that will fade away, but we do it for an eternal prize.

1 Corinthians 9:25 NLT

The Book of Proverbs tells us that self-control and patience are very good things to have. But for most of us, self-control and patience can also be very hard things to learn.

Are you having trouble being patient? And are you having trouble slowing down long enough to think before you act? If so, remember that self-control takes practice, and lots of it, so keep trying. And if you make a mistake, don't be too upset. After all, if you're going to be a really patient person, you shouldn't just be patient with others; you should also be patient with yourself.

TODAY'S PRAYER

Dear Lord, the Bible says that I should behave myself. Help me to control myself now, tomorrow, and every day of my life. Amen

WHEN YOU DON'T KNOW
WHAT TO SAY

Watch the way you talk. Let nothing foul or dirty come out of your mouth. Say only what helps, each word a gift.

Ephesians 4:29 MSG

Sometimes, it's hard to know exactly what to say. And sometimes, it can be very tempting to say something that isn't true—or something that isn't nice. But when you say things you shouldn't say, you'll regret it later.

So make this promise to yourself, and keep it—promise to think about the things you say before you say them. And whatever you do, always tell the truth. When you do these things, you'll be doing yourself a big favor, and you'll be obeying the Word of God.

TODAY'S PRAYER

Dear Lord, today and every day, I will try my best to say things that are pleasing to You and helpful to others. Amen

Do Yourself a Favor: Be Quick to Forgive

And whenever you stand praying, if you have anything against anyone, forgive him, so that your Father in heaven may also forgive you your wrongdoing.

Mark 11:25 HCSB

When you forgive somebody else, you're actually doing yourself a favor. Why? Because when you forgive the other person, you get rid of angry feelings that can make you unhappy.

Are you still angry about something that happened yesterday, or the day before that, or the day before that? Do yourself a big favor: forgive everybody (including yourself, if necessary). When you do, you won't change what happened yesterday, but you will make today a whole lot better.

TODAY'S PRAYER

Dear Lord, You have forgiven me. Now, it's my turn to forgive others. Help me fill my heart with kind thoughts, and help me fill each day with good deeds. Thank You, Lord, for Your love, for Your forgiveness, and for Your Son, Jesus. Amen

DAY 191

Sharing God's Love

It is good and pleasant when God's people live together in peace!

Psalm 133:1 NCV

A re your friends kind to you? And, are your friends nice to other people, too? If so, congratulations! If not, it's probably time to start looking for a few new friends. After all, it's really not very much fun to be around people who aren't nice to everybody.

The Bible teaches that a pure heart is a wonderful blessing. It's up to each of us to fill our hearts with love for God, love for Jesus, and love for all people. When we do, we feel better about ourselves.

Do you want to be the best person you can be? Then invite the love of Christ into your heart and share His love with your family and friends. And remember that lasting love always comes from a pure heart . . . like yours!

TODAY'S PRAYER

Dear Lord, I thank You for friends who help me feel better about myself. Help me to choose my friends wisely, and help me to treat my friends like I want them to treat me. Amen

DAY 192

KIND WORDS ARE BEST

Always be humble, gentle, and patient, accepting each other in love.

Ephesians 4:2 NCV

The Bible tells us that gentle words are helpful and that cruel words are not. But sometimes, especially when we're upset, our words and our actions may not be so gentle. Sometimes, we may say things that are unkind or hurtful to others. But it's wrong to hurt others.

So the next time you're tempted to say something or do something in a fit of anger, don't. And while you're at it, remember that gentle words are better than angry words and good deeds are better than the other kind. Always!

TODAY'S PRAYER

Dear Lord, the Bible teaches me to be gentle and kind. So, I will do my best to treat other people just like I want to be treated. Amen

DAY 193

GOD'S PROMISE OF LOVE

His banner over me was love.

Song of Solomon 2:4 KJV

In the Bible, God makes this amazing promise—He promises that He loves you. And it's a promise that He intends to keep.

No matter where you are (and no matter what you've done), you're never beyond the reach of God's love. So take time today (and every day) to thank Him for love that is too big to understand with your head, but not too big to feel with your heart.

A VERY VEGGIE BRIGHT IDEA

The life of faith is a daily exploration of the constant and countless ways in which God's grace and love are experienced.

Eugene Peterson

TODAY'S PRAYER

Dear Lord, the Bible teaches me that You are my loving Father. I thank You, Lord, for Your love and for Your Son. Amen

DAY 194

Very Big ideas about Patience

To start your day, take a few minutes to talk to your mom or dad about what these two quotations mean.

We must learn to wait.
There is grace supplied to
the one who waits.

Mrs. Charles E. Cowman

In the Bible, patience is not a passive
acceptance of circumstances.
It is a courageous perseverance in
the face of suffering and difficulty.

Warren Wiersbe

TODAY'S PRAYER

Dear Lord, sometimes it's hard to be patient, and that's exactly when I should try my hardest to be patient. Help me to obey You by being a patient, loving person . . . even when it's hard. Amen

TALK TO GOD EVERY DAY

Stay clear of silly stories that get dressed up as religion. Exercise daily in God—no spiritual flabbiness, please!

1 Timothy 4:7 MSG

Want to know God better? Then schedule a meeting with Him every day.

Each day has 1,440 minutes—will you spend a few of those minutes with your Heavenly Father? He deserves that much of your time and more. God wants you to pay attention to Him. So, if you haven't already done so, form the habit of spending quality time with your Creator. He deserves it . . . and so, for that matter, do you.

TODAY'S PRAYER

Dear Lord, I know that it's important to talk to You every day. And that's exactly what I will do. Amen

DAY 196

Don't Exaggerate

I have no greater joy than this: to hear that my children are walking in the truth.

3 John 1:4 HCSB

Perhaps you've heard the story of the boy who cried "wolf!" In that story, the boy exaggerated his problems and eventually got himself into BIG trouble!

When we pretend that our troubles are worse than they really are, we may earn a little sympathy now, but we'll invite lots of trouble later.

If you're ever tempted to cry wolf, don't. Exaggeration wasn't good for the boy who cried wolf, and it's not good for you.

A TIP TO START YOUR DAY

Don't exaggerate! All of us have enough troubles without pretending that we have more.

TODAY'S PRAYER

Dear Lord, I know that I should always tell the truth. And, I know that it's wrong to exaggerate my problems. Help me remember, Lord, that honesty is always the best policy. Amen

DAY 197

TRY TO MEMORIZE THIS VERSE

Trust in the Lord with all your heart,
and lean not on your own understanding;
in all your ways acknowledge Him,
and He shall direct your paths.

Proverbs 3:5-6 NKJV

This is an important Bible verse. Practice saying it
several times. And then, talk to your mom or dad
about exactly what the verse means . . .

A TIP FOR PARENTS
Today, talk to your child about . . . trusting God.

TODAY'S PRAYER
Dear Lord, I know that this world is in Your
hands. And, I know that You love me. Today, I
will trust You, I will praise You, and I will do my
best to follow in the footsteps of Your Son.
Amen

DAY 198

DON'T GROW TIRED OF FORGIVING

Then Peter came to him and asked, "Lord, how often should I forgive someone who sins against me? Seven times?" "No!" Jesus replied, "seventy times seven!"

Matthew 18:21-22 NLT

How often does God forgive us? More times than we can count! And that, by the way, is exactly how many times that God expects us to forgive other people—more times than we care to count.

Of this you can be sure: God won't ever get tired of forgiving you. And, because He has forgiven you, He doesn't want you to get tired of forgiving other people . . . ever!

TODAY'S PRAYER

Dear Lord, please give me the wisdom to forgive other people. You have forgiven me, Father, and I will be quick to forgive, too. Amen

DAY 199

TRY TO MEMORIZE THIS VERSE

*May the words of my mouth
and the meditation of my heart
be pleasing in your sight, O LORD,
my Rock and my Redeemer.*

Psalm 19:14 NIV

*This is an important Bible verse. Practice saying it
several times. And then, talk to your mom or dad
about exactly what the verse means . . .*

A TIP FOR PARENTS

Today, talk to your child about . . . pleasing God.

TODAY'S PRAYER

Dear Lord, You have given me too many blessings
to count. Today, tomorrow, and every day after
that, I will try to please You by doing good
deeds and thinking good thoughts. Amen

DAY 200

How Does Jesus Want You to Behave?

I've laid down a pattern for you. What I've done, you do.

John 13:15 MSG

If you're not certain whether something is right or wrong, remember to ask yourself this simple question: "What would Jesus do if He were here?" The answer to that question will tell you how to behave yourself.

Jesus was perfect, but we are not. Still, we must try as hard as we can to be like Him. When we do, we will love others, just like Christ loves us.

A TIP TO START YOUR DAY

Want to know what Jesus would do? Then learn what Jesus did!

TODAY'S PRAYER

Lord, when I am uncertain what to do, let me look to Jesus as my example. Let me do my best to behave like Jesus would behave if He were in my place. Thank You, Lord, for a perfect example of the perfect way to behave; that example is Your Son. Amen

DAY 201

WHAT a FRIEND You Have in Jesus!

Just as the Father has loved Me, I have also loved you; abide in My love.

John 15:9 NASB

D o you know that Jesus loves you? And have you thought about exactly what His love should mean to you? Well, Christ's love should make you feel better about your life, your family, your future, and yourself.

There's an old song that says, "What a friend we have in Jesus." Those words are certainly true! When you invite Him into your heart, Jesus will be your friend forever.

Jesus wants you to have a happy, healthy life. He wants you to behave yourself, and He wants you to feel good about yourself. And now, it's up to you to do your best to live up to the hopes and dreams of your very best friend: Jesus.

TODAY'S PRAYER

Dear Lord, I know that Jesus loves me. Thank You, Father, for sending Your Son to save the world and to save me. Amen

Learning to Share

Be generous: Invest in acts of charity. Charity yields high returns.

Ecclesiastes 11:1 MSG

Lots of people in the world aren't as fortunate as you are. Some of these folks live in faraway places, and that makes it harder to help them. But other people who need your help are living very near you.

Ask your parents to help you find ways to do something nice for folks who need it. And don't forget that everybody needs love, kindness, and respect, so you should always be ready to share those things, too.

A VERY VEGGIE BRIGHT IDEA

Success has nothing to do with what you gain in life or accomplish for yourself. It's what you do for others.

Danny Thomas

TODAY'S PRAYER

Dear God, You've given me a conscience that tells me right from wrong. Let me trust my conscience, and let me live according to Your teachings every day of my life. Amen

DAY 203

SHOWING PEOPLE WHAT IT MEANS TO FOLLOW JESUS

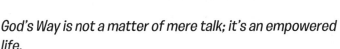

God's Way is not a matter of mere talk; it's an empowered life.

1 Corinthians 4:20 MSG

I f you're a good Christian, you should also be a good example to your friends and family members. Telling people about Jesus isn't enough. Your behavior should speak at least as loudly as your words.

Max Lucado writes, "In our faith we follow in someone's steps. In our faith we leave footprints to guide others. It's the principle of discipleship."

God wants you to guide others. And, you should want the same thing.

A VERY VEGGIE BRIGHT IDEA

A good example is the best sermon.

Thomas Fuller

TODAY'S PRAYER

Lord, make me a good example to my family and friends. And, let my words and my actions show people how my life has been changed by You.

Be Cheerful!

Jacob said, "For what a relief it is to see your friendly smile. It is like seeing the smile of God!"

Genesis 33:10 NLT

The Bible tells us that a cheerful heart is like medicine: it makes us feel better. Where does cheerfulness begin? It begins inside each of us; it begins in the heart. So let's be thankful to God for His blessings, and let's show our thanks by sharing good cheer wherever we go.

So, make sure that you share a smile and a kind word with as many people as you can. This old world needs all the cheering up it can get . . . and so do your friends.

TODAY'S PRAYER

Dear Lord, the Bible reminds me that this is the day You have made. Let me be a joyful Christian, Lord, quick to smile . . . slow to frown. And let me share Your love with my family and friends. Amen

DAY 205

IT'S GOOD TO ENCOURAGE OTHERS

So encourage each other and give each other strength, just as you are doing now.

1 Thessalonians 5:11 NCV

When other people are sad, what can we do? We can do our best to cheer them up by showing kindness and love.

The Bible tells us that we must care for each other, and when everybody is happy, that's an easy thing to do. But, when people are sad, for whatever reason, it's up to us to speak a kind word or to offer a helping hand.

Do you know someone who is discouraged or sad? If so, perhaps it's time to take matters into your own hands. Think of something you can do to cheer that person up . . . and then do it! You'll make two people happy.

TODAY'S PRAYER

Dear Lord, let me celebrate the victories of others. Help me make my family and friends feel better. Teach me how to encourage other people. And let my words and actions be worthy of Your Son. Amen

DAY 206

TRY TO MEMORIZE THIS VERSE

*I remind you to keep ablaze
the gift of God that is in you.*

2 Timothy 1:6 HCSB

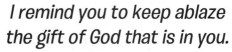

*This is an important Bible verse. Practice saying it
several times. And then, talk to your mom or dad
about exactly what the verse means . . .*

A TIP FOR PARENTS

Today, talk to your child about . . .
using the gifts God gives.

TODAY'S PRAYER

Dear Lord, You have given me so many gifts, and I am so
very grateful for all those blessings. Please help me use
my gifts, Lord, and let me help my friends use theirs. Amen

When Things Go Wrong

But as for you, be strong; don't be discouraged, for your work has a reward.

2 Chronicles 15:7 HCSB

Some days are more wonderful than other days. Sometimes, everything seems to go right, and on other days, many things seem to go wrong. But here's something to remember: even when you're disappointed with the way things turn out, God is near . . . and He loves you very much!

If you're disappointed, worried, sad, or afraid, you can talk to your parents and to God. And you will certainly feel better when you do!

TODAY'S PRAYER

Dear Lord, when I become upset, I'll remember that You have the power to make everything better. Whatever happens, Lord, I'll trust You to protect me. And when things don't work out, I'll wait patiently for You to make things better. Amen

DAY 208

GOD ALWAYS KNOWS BEST

However, each one must live his life in the situation the Lord assigned when God called him.

1 Corinthians 7:17 HCSB

Here are three things to think about today: 1. God loves you. 2. God wants what's best for you. 3. God has a plan for you.

God's plan may not always happen exactly like you want, but remember: God always knows best. Sometimes, even though you may want something very badly, you must still be patient and wait for the right time to get it. And the right time, of course, is determined by God.

Even if you don't get exactly what you want today, you can be sure that God wants what's best for you . . . today, tomorrow, and forever.

A TIP TO START YOUR DAY

God has a plan for the world and for you. When you discover His plan for your life–and when you follow in the footsteps of His Son–you will be rewarded.

TODAY'S PRAYER

Dear Lord, You have a plan for this world and a plan for me. Help me to follow Your plan and obey Your commandments now and forever. Amen

DAY 209

Very Big ideas about Behaving Yourself

To start your day, take a few minutes to talk to your mom or dad about what these two quotations mean.

Do nothing that you would not like
to be doing when Jesus comes.
Go no place where you would not like
to be found when He returns.

Corrie ten Boom

Life is a series of choices between
the bad, the good, and the best.
Everything depends on how we choose.

Vance Havner

TODAY'S PRAYER

Dear Lord, when I'm tempted to do the wrong thing, help me to slow down and to think about my behavior. And then, help me to know what's right and to do what's right. Amen

VERY BIG IDEAS ABOUT ASKING GOD FOR THE THINGS YOU NEED

To start your day, take a few minutes to talk to your mom or dad about what these two quotations mean.

Some people think God does not like to be troubled with our constant asking. But, the way to trouble God is not to come at all.

D. L. Moody

Don't be afraid to ask your heavenly Father for anything you need. Indeed, nothing is too small for God's attention or too great for his power.

Dennis Swanberg

TODAY'S PRAYER

Dear Lord, the Bible teaches me that pleasing people is not nearly as important as pleasing You. Let me please You, Lord, now and always. Amen

ALWAYS BE KIND

Therefore, God's chosen ones, holy and loved, put on heartfelt compassion, kindness, humility, gentleness, and patience.

Colossians 3:12 HCSB

How hard is it to say a kind word? Not very! Yet sometimes we're so busy that we forget to say the very things that might make other people feel better.

We should always try to say nice things to our families and friends. And when we feel like saying something that's not so nice, perhaps we should stop and think before we say it. Kind words help; cruel words hurt. It's as simple as that. And, when we say the right thing at the right time, we give a gift that can change someone's day or someone's life.

TODAY'S PRAYER

Dear Lord, I know the Bible teaches me to treat other people like I want to be treated. So, help me show kindness to everybody I meet. Amen

DAY 212

God's Love for You is Real

For the LORD your God has arrived to live among you. He is a mighty savior. He will rejoice over you with great gladness. With his love, he will calm all your fears. He will exult over you by singing a happy song.

Zephaniah 3:17 NLT

How big is God's love for you? As long as you're alive, you'll never be able to figure it out because God's love is just too big to understand. But this much we know: God loves you so much that He sent His Son, Jesus, to come to this earth so you could live forever in heaven.

God's love is bigger and more powerful than anybody can imagine, but His love is very real. So do yourself a favor right now: accept God's love with open arms and welcome His Son, Jesus, into your heart. When you do, your life will be changed today, tomorrow, and forever.

TODAY'S PRAYER

Dear Lord, thank You for loving me. You sent Jesus to this earth so that I can live forever in heaven. Thank You, Father, for Your Son and for Your love. Amen

DAY 213

Promises You Can Depend On

Do not be afraid or discouraged. For the LORD your God is with you wherever you go.

Joshua 1:9 NLT

God has made quite a few promises to you, and He intends to keep every single one of them. You will find these promises in a book like no other: the Holy Bible. The Bible is your map for life here on earth and for life in heaven.

God's promises never fail and they never grow old. You must trust those promises and share them with your family, with your friends, and with the world . . . starting now . . . and ending never.

A TIP TO START YOUR DAY

God keeps His promises to you, so make sure that you keep your promises to Him.

TODAY'S PRAYER

Dear God, the Bible contains many promises. I thank You for those promises, Father, and I will trust them now and forever. Amen

DAY 214

How to Be Happy

I will praise you, Lord, with all my heart. I will tell all the miracles you have done. I will be happy because of you; God Most High, I will sing praises to your name.

Psalm 9:1-2 NCV

Do you want to be happy? Here are some things you should do: love God and His Son, Jesus; obey the Golden Rule; and always try to do the right thing. When you do these things, you'll discover that happiness goes hand-in-hand with good behavior. The happiest people do not misbehave; the happiest people are not cruel or greedy. The happiest people don't say unkind things. The happiest people are those who love God and follow his rules–starting, of course, with the Golden one.

TODAY'S PRAYER

Dear Lord, You have given me more blessings than I can count. I will do my best to be a joyful Christian, as I give thanks for Your blessings and for Your Son. Amen

DAY 215

VERY BIG IDEAS ABOUT KINDNESS

To start your day, take a few minutes to talk to your mom or dad about what these two quotations mean.

Keep your eyes open wide and your heart open wider.

Criswell Freeman

The attitude of kindness is everyday stuff like a great pair of sneakers. Not frilly. Not fancy. Just plain and comfortable.

Barbara Johnson

TODAY'S PRAYER

Dear Lord, I want to be a good person and a good Christian. Every day, I will do my best to be kind, helpful, and polite. When I do these things, I'll know that I'm walking in the footsteps of Your Son. Amen

DAY 216

Very Big ideas About Saying Thanks to God

To start your day, take a few minutes to talk to your mom or dad about what these two quotations mean.

Praise and thank God
for who He is and for
what He has done for you.

Billy Graham

When is the best time to say
"thanks" to God? Any time.
God loves you all the time,
and that's exactly why you should praise
Him all the time.

Criswell Freeman

TODAY'S PRAYER

Dear Lord, You have given me so many gifts, and I am so very grateful for all those blessings. Let me use my gifts, Lord, and let me help my friends use theirs. Amen

WISDOM ACCORDING TO GOD

Do not deceive yourselves. If any one of you thinks he is wise by the standards of this age, he should become a "fool" so that he may become wise. For the wisdom of this world is foolishness in God's sight.

1 Corinthians 3:18-19 NIV

If you look in a dictionary, you'll see that the word "wisdom" means "using good judgement, and knowing what is true." But there's more: it's not just enough to know what's right; if you really want to become a wise person, you must also do what's right.

A big part of "doing what's right" is learning self-control . . . and the best day to start learning self-control is this one!

TODAY'S PRAYER

Dear Lord, I trust Your wisdom. The most important wisdom is Yours and the most important truth is Yours. Now and always, I will show my respect for You by obeying Your commandments. Amen

DAY 218

God's Love is Meant to Be Shared

And we have known and believed the love that God has for us. God is love, and he who abides in love abides in God, and God in him.

1 John 4:16 NKJV

The Bible tells us that God is love and that if we wish to know Him, we must have love in our hearts. Sometimes, of course, when we're tired, angry, or frustrated, it is very hard for us to be loving. Thankfully, anger and frustration are feelings that come and go, but God's love lasts forever.

If you'd like to improve your day and your life, share God's love with your family and friends. Every time you love, and every time you give, God smiles.

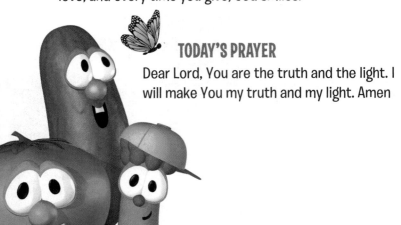

TODAY'S PRAYER

Dear Lord, You are the truth and the light. I will make You my truth and my light. Amen

God's Greatest Promise

I assure you: Anyone who believes has eternal life.

John 6:47 HCSB

It's time to remind yourself of a promise that God made a long time ago—the promise that God sent His Son Jesus to save the world and to save you! And when you stop to think about it, there can be no greater promise than that.

No matter where you are, God is with you. God loves you, and He sent His Son so that you can live forever in heaven with your loved ones. WOW! That's the greatest promise in the history of the universe. The End.

A TIP TO START YOUR DAY

God's gift of eternal life is amazing. Talk to your friends about God's promise of eternal life and what that promise means to you.

TODAY'S PRAYER

Dear Lord, Jesus died so that I can live forever with Him in heaven. Thank You, Father, for Your Son and for the priceless gift of eternal life. Amen

DAY 220

Make Time for God every Day

Every morning he wakes me. He teaches me to listen like a student. The Lord God helps me learn . . .

Isaiah 50:4-5 NCV

Where does God fit into your life? Do you "squeeze Him in" on Sundays and at mealtimes? Or do you talk to Him more often than that?

Even if you're the busiest kid on the planet, you can still make time for God. And when you think about it, isn't that the very least you should do?

A VERY VEGGIE BRIGHT IDEA

We all need to make time for God. Even Jesus made time to be alone with the Father.

Kay Arthur

TODAY'S PRAYER

Dear Lord, it's always a good time to pray, and it's always a good time to learn about Jesus. So I'll talk to You often, Lord, and I'll trust Your promises today, tomorrow, and every day. Amen

Keep God in Your Heart

Create in me a pure heart, God, and make my spirit right again.

Psalm 51:10 NCV

O ther people see you from the outside. God sees you from the inside–God sees your heart.

Kindness comes from the heart. So does sharing. So if you want to show your family and your friends that your heart is filled with kindness and love, one way to do it is by sharing. But don't worry about trying to show God what kind of person you are. He already knows your heart, and He loves you more than you can imagine.

A VERY VEGGIE BRIGHT IDEA

The God who dwells in heaven is willing to dwell also in the heart of the humble believer.

Warren Wiersbe

TODAY'S PRAYER

Dear Lord, You know my heart. Today, tomorrow, and every day after that, let me think things and do things that are pleasing to You. Amen

DAY 222

TRY TO MEMORIZE THIS VERSE

I can do all things through Christ which strengtheneth me.

Philippians 4:13 KJV

This is an important Bible verse about Jesus. Practice saying it several times. And then, talk to your mom or dad about exactly what the verse means . . .

A TIP FOR PARENTS
Today, talk to your child about . . .
the strength Christ gives.

TODAY'S PRAYER
Dear Lord, when I give my heart to You, I become better and stronger. Thank You, Lord, for filling my heart with strength, with hope, and with love. Amen

DAY 223

Honesty Begins at Home

Good people will be guided by honesty.

Proverbs 11:3 ICB

Should you be honest with your parents? Certainly. With your brothers and sisters? Of course. With cousins, grandparents, aunts and uncles? Yes! In fact, you should be honest with everybody in your family because honesty starts at home.

If you can't be honest in your own house, how can you expect to be honest in other places, like at church or at school? So make sure that you're completely honest with your family. If you are, then you're much more likely to be honest with everybody else.

A TIP TO START YOUR DAY

If you're tempted to say something that isn't true, don't say anything. A closed mouth tells no lies.

TODAY'S PRAYER

Dear Lord, help me be honest with everybody, especially my parents. They need to hear the truth from me, and I need to be truthful with them, today, tomorrow, and every day after that. Amen

DAY 224

Be Joyful!

Always be full of joy in the Lord. I say it again—rejoice!

Philippians 4:4 NLT

A man named C. S. Lewis once said, "Joy is the serious business of heaven." And he was right! God seriously wants you to be a seriously joyful person.

One way that you can have a more joyful life is by learning how to become a more obedient person. When you do, you'll stay out of trouble, and you'll have lots more time for fun.

So here's a way to be a more joyful, happy person: do the right thing! It's the best way to live.

A VERY VEGGIE BRIGHT IDEA

Joy comes not from what we have but from what we are.

C. H. Spurgeon

TODAY'S PRAYER

Dear Lord, I am thankful for all Your blessings. I will be a happy Christian, Father, as I share Your joy with my friends, with my family, and with the world. Amen

SHARING LOVE AND KINDNESS

Talk and act like a person expecting to be judged by the Rule that sets us free. For if you refuse to act kindly, you can hardly expect to be treated kindly. Kind mercy wins over harsh judgment every time.

James 2:12-13 MSG

Where does kindness start? It starts in our hearts and works its way out from there. Jesus taught us that a pure heart is a wonderful blessing. It's up to each of us to fill our hearts with love for God, love for Jesus, and love for all people. When we do, we are blessed.

Do you want to be the best person you can be? Then invite the love of Christ into your heart and share His love with your family and friends. And remember that lasting love always comes from a pure heart . . . like yours!

TODAY'S PRAYER

Dear Lord, I want to be helpful and kind. When I say what's right and do what's right, I feel better about myself. So I'll say kind things and do kind things every day. Amen

DAY 226

Forming New Habits

For every tree is known by its own fruit.

Luke 6:44 NKJV

Perhaps you've tried to change something about yourself, but you're still falling back into your old habits. If so, don't get discouraged. Instead, become even more determined to become the person God wants you to be.

If you trust God, and if you keep asking Him to help you change bad habits, He will help you make yourself into a new person. So, if at first you don't succeed, keep praying. If you keep asking, you'll eventually get the answers you need.

A TIP TO START YOUR DAY

Choose your habits carefully: habits are easier to make than they are to break, so be careful!

TODAY'S PRAYER

Dear Lord, I'm growing up every day. Help me form good habits every day, too. Amen

DAY 227

The Most Important Book You'll Ever Own

All Scripture is inspired by God and is profitable for teaching, for rebuking, for correcting, for training in righteousness, so that the man of God may be complete, equipped for every good work.

2 Timothy 3:16-17 HCSB

D o you think about the Bible a lot . . . or not? Hopefully, you pay careful attention to the things you learn from God's Word! After all, the Bible is God's message to you. It's not just a book, it's a priceless, one-of-a-kind treasure . . . and it has amazing things to teach you. So start learning about the Bible now, and keep learning about it for as long as you live!

A TIP TO START YOUR DAY

Who's supposed to be taking care of your Bible? If it's you, then take very good care of it; it's by far the most important book you own!

TODAY'S PRAYER

Dear Lord, the Bible is Your gift to me. I will use it, I will trust it, and I will obey it, this day and every day that I live. Amen

DAY 228

TRY TO MEMORIZE THIS VERSE

But the fruit of the Spirit is love, joy, peace, patience, kindness, goodness, faith, gentleness, self-control. Against such things there is no law.

Galatians 5:22-23 HCSB

This is an important Bible verse. Practice saying it several times. And then, talk to your mom or dad about exactly what the verse means . . .

A TIP FOR PARENTS

Today, talk to your child about . . .
the fruits of the Spirit.

TODAY'S PRAYER

Dear Lord, help me become the kind of person who always lets Your Spirit live and grow in my heart. Amen

WHEN FRIENDS MISBEHAVE

Whoever walks with the wise will become wise; whoever walks with fools will suffer harm.

Proverbs 13:20 NLT

If you're like most people, you have probably been tempted to "go along with the crowd," even when the crowd was misbehaving. But here's something to think about: just because your friends may be misbehaving doesn't mean that you have to misbehave, too.

When people behave badly, they can spoil things in a hurry. So make sure that they don't spoil things for you.

So, if your friends misbehave, don't copy them! Instead, do the right thing. You'll be glad you did . . . and so will God!

A TIP TO START YOUR DAY

Remember that it's more important to be respected than to be liked. So, don't follow the crowd; follow your conscience!

TODAY'S PRAYER

Dear Lord, when I try please You, I'll make better choices. So I'll try my best to please You, Lord, now and forever. Amen

DAY 230

TRY TO MEMORIZE THIS VERSE

*For the wages of sin is death,
but the gift of God is eternal life
in Christ Jesus our Lord.*

Romans 6:23 NIV

*This is an important Bible verse. Practice saying it
several times. And then, talk to your mom or dad
about exactly what the verse means . . .*

A TIP FOR PARENTS
Today, talk to your child about . . .
God's promise of eternal life.

TODAY'S PRAYER
Dear Lord, the Bible promises that I will live forever
in heaven when I accept Your Son into my heart.
Thank You, Father, for Jesus and for the priceless
gift of eternal life. Amen

DAY 231

Living By God's Rules

Does the LORD delight in burnt offerings and sacrifices as much as in obeying the voice of the LORD? To obey is better than sacrifice . . .

1 Samuel 15:22 NIV

God has rules, and He wants you to obey them. He wants you to be fair, honest, and kind. He wants you to behave yourself, and He wants you to respect your parents. God has other rules, too, and you'll find them in a very special book: the Bible.

With a little help from your parents, you can figure out God's rules. And then, it's up to you to live by them. When you do, everybody will be pleased–you'll be pleased, your parents will be pleased . . . and God will be pleased, too.

TODAY'S PRAYER

Dear Lord, when I play by Your rules, You bless my life. But, when I disobey Your rules, I suffer the consequences. Help me obey You and my parents . . . starting right now! Amen

DAY 232

You Don't Have to Be Perfect

You're blessed when you're content with just who you are—no more, no less. That's the moment you find yourselves proud owners of everything that can't be bought.

Matthew 5:5 MSG

When God made you, He gave you special talents and opportunities that are yours and yours alone. That means you're a very special, one-of-a-kind person, but that doesn't mean that you should expect to be perfect. After all, only one earthly being ever lived life to perfection, and He was, of course, Jesus. And Jesus loves you even when you're not perfect. Your parents feel the same way. And if all those people love you, you should love yourself, too.

TODAY'S PRAYER

Dear Lord, I don't have to be perfect to please You. Thank You for Your love, Father, and for Your forgiveness, and for Your Son. Amen

DAY 233

Need More Patience?
Pray About It!

For the eyes of the Lord are over the righteous, and his ears are open unto their prayers: but the face of the Lord is against them that do evil.

1 Peter 3:12 KJV

Would you like to become a more patient boy? Then pray about it. Would you like to learn how to use better self-control? Then pray about it. Are you tempted to throw a temper tantrum? Pray about it.

Whenever you pray about something, God hears your prayer . . . and He can help. So don't worry about things; pray about them. God is waiting . . . and listening!

A TIP TO START YOUR DAY

Even when prayer does not change your circumstances, prayer is important because it changes you.

TODAY'S PRAYER

Dear Lord, thank You for loving me. I will return Your love by sharing it . . . today, tomorrow, and always. Amen

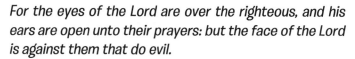

DAY 234

Listen to Your Parents

Listen carefully to wisdom; set your mind on understanding.

Proverbs 2:2 NCV

Are you the kind of boy who listens carefully to the things your parents tell you? You should. Your parents want the very best for you. They want you to be happy and healthy; they want you to be smart and to do smart things. Your parents have much to teach you, and you have much to learn. So listen carefully to the things your mom and dad have to say. And ask lots of questions. When you do, you'll soon discover that your parents have lots of answers . . . lots of very good answers.

A TIP TO START YOUR DAY

When in doubt, open your ears and close your mouth.

TODAY'S PRAYER

Dear Lord, let me listen respectfully to my parents, to my teachers, and to You. I have much to learn. Let me learn as much as I can as soon as I can, and let me be a good example for other people to follow. Amen

Learn from Your Mistakes!

If you hide your sins, you will not succeed. If you confess and reject them, you will receive mercy.

Proverbs 28:13 NCV

The Bible says that when people make mistakes, God corrects them. And that means that if you make a mistake, God will try to find a way to teach you how to keep from making that same mistake again.

God doesn't expect you to be perfect, but He does expect you to learn from your mistakes—NOW!

A TIP TO START YOUR DAY

When you make a mistake, learn something and forgive someone: yourself. Remember, you don't have to be perfect to be wonderful.

TODAY'S PRAYER

Dear Lord, sometimes I make mistakes, and when I do, please help me learn from them. Amen

DAY 236

TRY TO MEMORIZE THIS VERSE

God, your justice reaches to the skies.
You have done great things;
God, there is no one like you.

Psalm 71:19 NCV

This is an important Bible verse. Practice saying it several times. And then, talk to your mom or dad about exactly what the verse means . . .

A TIP FOR PARENTS

Today, talk to your child about . . .
God's power to do miraculous things.

TODAY'S PRAYER

Dear God, Your power is far too great for us to understand. But we can sense Your presence and Your love every day of our lives—and that's exactly what we will try to do! Amen

DAY 237

VERY BIG IDEAS ABOUT JESUS

To start your day, take a few minutes to talk to your mom or dad about what these two quotations mean.

What do you think God wants you to do? The answer is that He wants you to turn to Jesus and open your life to Him.

Billy Graham

Jesus: the proof of God's love.

Philip Yancey

TODAY'S PRAYER

Dear Lord, thank You for Your Son. Jesus loves me and He shares so much with me. Let me share His love with others so that through me, they can understand what it means to follow Him. Amen

DAY 238

TRY TO MEMORIZE THIS VERSE

*The righteous
will live by his faith.*

Habakkuk 2:4 NIV

*This is an important Bible verse about faith.
Practice saying it several times. And then,
talk to your mom or dad about exactly
what the verse means . . .*

A TIP FOR PARENTS

Today, talk to your child about . . .
the need to live by faith.

TODAY'S PRAYER

Dear Lord, help me strengthen my faith–and
share it–this day and every day of my life. Amen

Keep on Forgiving

You have heard that it was said, "Love your neighbor and hate your enemies." But I say to you, love your enemies. Pray for those who hurt you.

Matthew 5:43-44 NCV

I f you forgive somebody once, that's enough, right? WRONG!!! Even if you've forgiven somebody many times before, you must keep on forgiving.

Jesus teaches us that we must keep forgiving people even if they continue to misbehave. Why? Because we, too, need to be forgiven over and over again. And if God keeps forgiving us, then we must be willing to do the same thing for others.

A VERY VEGGIE BRIGHT IDEA

We must not only learn how to forgive; we must also learn how to keep forgiving.

Criswell Freeman

TODAY'S PRAYER

Dear Lord, the Bible teaches me to forgive other people, and that's what I will do today, tomorrow, and every day of my life. Amen

DAY 240

Your Amazing Talents!

Now there are varieties of gifts, but the same Spirit. And there are varieties of ministries, and the same Lord.

1 Corinthians 12:4-5 NASB

You've got very special talents, talents that have been given to you by God. So here's a question: Will you use your talents or not? God wants you to use your talents to become a better person and a better Christian. And that's what you should want for yourself.

As you're trying to figure out exactly what you're good at, be sure and talk about it with your parents. They can help you decide how best to use and improve the gifts God has given you.

A TIP TO START YOUR DAY

God gives you talents for a reason: to use them.

TODAY'S PRAYER

Lord, thank You for the talents You have given me. I will treasure those talents, and I will use them as I try my best to walk in the footsteps of Your Son. Amen

DAY 241

GUARD YOUR THOUGHTS

Set your minds on what is above, not on what is on the earth.

Colossians 3:2 HCSB

D o you try to think about things that are honorable, true, and pleasing to God? The Bible says that you should. Do you lift your hopes and your prayers to God many times each day? The Bible says that you should. Do you turn away from bad thoughts and bad people? The Bible says that you should.

The Bible instructs you to guard your thoughts against things that are hurtful or wrong. And when you turn away from the bad and turn instead toward God and His Son, Jesus, you will be protected and you will be blessed.

A TIP TO START YOUR DAY

Good thoughts lead to good deeds and bad thoughts lead elsewhere. So guard your thoughts accordingly.

TODAY'S PRAYER

Dear Lord, You are my Teacher. Help me to learn from You. And then, let me show others what it means to be a kind, generous, loving Christian. Amen

THE BEST TIME TO BE OBEDIENT

The one who has My commandments and keeps them is the one who loves Me. And the one who loves Me will be loved by My Father. I also will love him and will reveal Myself to him.

John 14:21 HCSB

When is the best time to be obedient? It's always the right time to obey your parents, your teachers, and your Father in heaven.

It's not enough to know what's right; if you really want to become a better person, you must also do what's right. Starting now, and stopping never.

A VERY VEGGIE BRIGHT IDEA

For better or worse, you will eventually become more and more like the people you associate with. So why not associate with people who make you better, not worse?

Marie T. Freeman

TODAY'S PRAYER

Dear Lord, You know what's best for me. Help me understand Your rules and obey them, today, tomorrow, and every day after that. Amen

DAY 243

Patience and the Golden Rule

Always be humble and gentle. Be patient and accept each other with love.

Ephesians 4:2 ICB

Jesus gave us a Golden Rule for living: He said that we should treat other people in the same way that we want to be treated. And because we want other people to be patient with us, we, in turn, must be patient with them.

Being patient with other people means treating them with kindness, respect, and understanding. It means waiting our turn when we're standing in line and forgiving our friends when they've done something we don't like. Sometimes, it's hard to be patient, but we've got to do our best. And when we do, we're following the Golden Rule–God's rule for how to treat others–and everybody wins!

TODAY'S PRAYER

Dear Lord, let me be patient with other people, just as You've been patient with me. Amen

DAY 244

Don't Judge!

Don't pick on people, jump on their failures, criticize their faults–unless, of course, you want the same treatment. That critical spirit has a way of boomeranging.

Matthew 7:1-2 MSG

Here's something worth thinking about: if you judge other people harshly, God will judge you in the same way. But that's not all (thank goodness!). The Bible also promises that if you forgive other people, you, too, will be forgiven.

Are you tempted to blame people, criticize people, or judge people? If so, remember this: God is already judging what people do, and He doesn't need–or want–your help.

A TIP TO START YOUR DAY

God has the wisdom to judge other people, but you don't. So don't be too quick to judge.

TODAY'S PRAYER

Dear Lord, the Bible teaches me that it's wrong to judge other people. So, I'll be slow to judge and quick to be kind. Amen

DAY 245

Sharing Begins at Home

A person who gives to others will get richer. Whoever helps others will himself be helped.

Proverbs 11:25 ICB

A good place to start sharing is at home—but it isn't always an easy place to start. Sometimes, especially when we're tired or mad, we don't treat our family members as nicely as we should. And that's too bad!

Do you have brothers and sisters? Or cousins? If so, you're lucky.

Sharing your things—without whining or complaining—is a wonderful way to show your family that you love them. So the next time a brother or sister or cousin asks to borrow something, say "yes" without getting mad. It's a great way to say, "I love you."

TODAY'S PRAYER

Dear Lord, the Bible teaches me to share. So, Father, help me remember the importance of sharing my things, my prayers, and my love with family members and friends. Amen

DAY 246

You're Special

To acquire wisdom is to love oneself; people who cherish understanding will prosper.

Proverbs 19:8 NLT

How many boys in the world are exactly like you? Only one—the boy you see every time you look in the mirror. In other words, the only person in the world who's exactly like you . . . IS YOU! And that means you're special: special to God, special to your family, special to your friends, and a special addition to God's wonderful world!

The Bible says that God made you in "an amazing and wonderful way." So the next time that you start feeling like you don't measure up, remember this: when God made all the people of the earth, He only made one you. And that means you're a V.I.P. And what is a V.I.P.? A "Very Important Person," of course.

TODAY'S PRAYER

Dear Lord, You only made one me, and I know that You love me very, very much. I thank You for Your love, Lord, and I thank You for the gift of Your Son, Jesus. Amen

DAY 247

Use Your Ears!

My dearly loved brothers, understand this: everyone must be quick to hear, slow to speak, and slow to anger.

James 1:19 HCSB

When God made you, He gave you two ears and one mouth for a very good reason: you can learn at least twice as much by listening as you can by talking. That's why it's usually better to listen first and talk second. But when you're frustrated or tired, it's easy to speak first and think later.

A big part of growing up is learning how to slow down long enough to listen to the things that people have to say. So the next time you're tempted to turn off your ears and tune up your mouth, stop, listen, and think. After all, God gave you two wonderful ears for a very good reason: to use them.

A TIP TO START YOUR DAY

Try to listen as much as (or more than) you speak.

TODAY'S PRAYER

Dear Lord, I have lots to learn. Help me to watch, to listen, to think, and to learn, every day of my life. Amen

DAY 248

Very Big Ideas About Waiting Your Turn

To start your day, take a few minutes to talk to your mom or dad about what these two quotations mean.

If only we could be as patient with other people as God is with us!

Jim Gallery

God gave everyone patience— wise people use it.

Anonymous

TODAY'S PRAYER

Lord, sometimes it's hard to be a patient person, and that's exactly when I should try my hardest to be patient. Help me to be patient and kind, even when it's hard. Amen

DAY 249

REAL FAITH

But whoever keeps His word, truly in him the love of God is perfected. This is how we know we are in Him: the one who says he remains in Him should walk just as He walked.

1 John 2:5-6 HCSB

Jesus wants to have a real relationship with you. Are you willing to have a real friendship with Him? Unless you can answer this question with a resounding "Yes!" you may miss out on some wonderful things.

Every day offers yet another opportunity to behave yourself like a real Christian. When you do, God will guide your steps and bless your endeavors . . . forever.

A VERY VEGGIE BRIGHT IDEA

Think of this—we may live together with Jesus here and now, a daily walking with Him.

Elisabeth Elliot

TODAY'S PRAYER

Dear Lord, I know that You sent Jesus to save the world and to save me. I thank You, Father, for Your Son, and I will do my best to follow Him, now and forever. Amen

Rejoice Today!

Shout with joy to the LORD, O earth! Worship the LORD with gladness. Come before him, singing with joy.

Psalm 100:1-2 NLT

Have you made the choice to rejoice? Hopefully so. After all, if you're a Christian, you have plenty of reasons to be joyful.

So today, think about this: God has given you too many blessings to count, but you can certainly count some of those blessings. Your job is to honor God with your prayers, your words, your behavior, and your joy.

A VERY VEGGIE BRIGHT IDEA

According to Jesus, it is God's will that His children be filled with the joy of life.

Catherine Marshall

TODAY'S PRAYER

Dear Lord, I will be joyful. I will celebrate the life You have given me, and I will try my best to help other people celebrate their lives, too. Amen

THE BEST TIME TO PRAISE GOD

The LORD is my strength and song, and He has become my salvation; He is my God, and I will praise Him.

Exodus 15:2 NIV

When is the best time to praise God? In church? Before dinner is served? At bedtime? None of the above. The best time to praise God is all day, every day, to the greatest extent we can, with thanksgiving in our hearts, and with a song on our lips. Dr. Wayne Oates once admitted, "Many of my prayers are made with my eyes open. You see, it seems I'm always praying about something, and it's not always convenient–or safe–to close my eyes." Dr. Oates understood that God always hears our prayers and that the position of our eyelids is of no concern to Him.

So, find a little more time to lift your concerns to God in prayer, and praise Him for all that He has done. Whether your eyes are open or closed, He's listening.

TODAY'S PRAYER

Dear Lord, today and every day I will praise You. I will praise You, Father, with my thoughts, my prayers, my words, and my actions . . . now and forever. Amen

DAY 252

THE GOLDEN RULE FOR LIVING AND FORGIVING

Therefore, whatever you want others to do for you, do also the same for them—this is the Law and the Prophets.

Matthew 7:12 HCSB

The words of Matthew 7:12 remind us that, as believers in Christ, we should treat others as we wish to be treated. This is called the Golden Rule, but for Christians, it's worth much more than gold.

Do you want other people to forgive you when you make mistakes? Of course you do. And that's why you should be willing to forgive them.

The Golden Rule should be your tool for deciding how you will treat others. So use the Golden Rule as your guide for living and forgiving!

TODAY'S PRAYER

Dear Lord, I know that whenever I ask for forgiveness, You give it. Thank You, Father, for forgiving me when I make mistakes. Today and always, I will be quick to forgive others, just as You have forgiven me. Amen

DAY 253

GOD SEES THE HEART

God does not see the same way people see. People look at the outside of a person, but the Lord looks at the heart.

1 Samuel 16:7 NCV

O ther people see you from the outside, and sometimes people will judge you by the way you look. But God doesn't care how you look on the outside. Why? Because God is wiser than that; God cares about what you are on the inside–God sees your heart.

If you're like most people, you'll worry a little bit about the way you look (or maybe you worry a lot about it). But please don't worry too much about your appearance!

How you look on the outside isn't important . . . but how you feel on the inside is important. So don't worry about trying to impress other people. Instead of trying to impress other kids, try to impress God by being the best person you can be.

TODAY'S PRAYER

Dear Lord, my friends see me from the outside, but You see my heart. And, it's what's inside my heart that matters most. So, let me worry less about the way I appear and more about the way I behave. Amen

DAY 254

Choices Matter

The thing you should want most is God's kingdom and doing what God wants. Then all these other things you need will be given to you.

Matthew 6:33 NCV

There's really no way to get around it: choices matter. If you make good choices, good things will usually happen to you. And if you make bad choices, bad things will usually happen.

The next time you have an important choice to make, ask yourself this: "Am I doing what God wants me to do?" If you can answer that question with a great big "YES," then go ahead. But if you're not sure the choice you are about to make is right, slow down. Why? Because choices matter . . . a lot!

TODAY'S PRAYER

Dear God, every day I have so many choices to make. Help me make good choices by following in the footsteps of Your Son, Jesus. Amen

DAY 255

Be Kind. Don't Gossip!

So rid yourselves of all wickedness, all deceit, hypocrisy, envy, and all slander.

1 Peter 2:1 HCSB

D o you know what gossip is? It's when we say bad things about people who are not around. When we gossip, we hurt others and we hurt ourselves. That's why the Bible tells us that gossip is wrong.

Sometimes, it's tempting to say bad things about people, and when we do, it makes us feel important . . . for a while. But, after a while, the bad things that we say come back to hurt us, and of course they hurt other people, too. So if you want to be a kind person and a good friend, don't gossip . . . and don't listen to people who do.

TODAY'S PRAYER

Dear Lord, if other people say things that are hurtful, I won't join in. Today and every day, I will try my best to say things that are helpful and kind, not harmful or rude. Amen

Lend a Helping Hand

Never walk away from someone who deserves help; your hand is God's hand for that person.

Proverbs 3:27 MSG

Sometimes we would like to help make the world a better place, but we're not sure how to do it. Jesus told the story of the "Good Samaritan," a man who helped a fellow traveler when no one else would. We, too, should be good Samaritans when we find people who need our help. A good place to start helping other people is at home . . . and of course, at school and at church.

Another way that we can help other people is to pray for them. God always hears our prayers, so we should talk with Him as often as we can. When we do, we're not only doing a wonderful thing for the people we pray for, we're also doing a wonderful thing for ourselves, too. Why? Because we feel better about ourselves when we're helping other people. And the more we help others, the better we should feel about ourselves.

TODAY'S PRAYER

Dear Lord, let me help others in every way that I can. Jesus served others; I can too. I will serve other people with my good deeds and with my prayers, and I will give thanks for all those who serve and protect our nation and our world. Amen

Look Before You Leap

Enthusiasm without knowledge is not good. If you act too quickly, you might make a mistake.

Proverbs 19:2 NCV

A re you sometimes just a little bit impulsive? Do you sometimes fail to look before you leap? If so, God wants you to be a little bit more careful–or maybe a lot more careful!

The Bible makes it clear: we're supposed to behave wisely, not carelessly. But sometimes we're tempted to rush ahead and do things before we think about them.

So do yourself a big favor–slow down, think things through, and look carefully before you leap.

TODAY'S PRAYER

Dear Lord, sometimes I'm in a hurry. When I'm tempted to rush, help me slow down and think about the things I'm about to do before I do them. Amen

DAY 258

Forgiveness Can Be Hard

Anyone who claims to live in God's light and hates a brother or sister is still in the dark.

1 John 2:9 MSG

God tells us that we must forgive other people, even when we'd rather not. So, if you're angry with anybody (or if you're upset by something you yourself have done), it's time to forgive. Right now!

But what if you have already tried to forgive somebody yet simply can't do it? Then you must keep trying. If you can't seem to forgive someone, you should keep asking God to help you until you do. And you can be sure of this: if you keep asking for God's help, He will give it.

A TIP TO START YOUR DAY

Because God has forgiven you, you can forgive everybody, including yourself.

TODAY'S PRAYER

Dear Lord, sometimes it's very hard to forgive those who have hurt me, but with Your help, I can forgive them. Help me to bring forgiveness into my heart, so that I can forgive others just as You have already forgiven me. Amen

DAY 259

KIND WORDS AND GOOD DEEDS MAKE OTHER PEOPLE FEEL BETTER

Be gracious in your speech. The goal is to bring out the best in others in a conversation, not put them down, not cut them out.

Colossians 4:6 MSG

Do you like for people to say kind words to you? Of course you do! And that's exactly how other people feel, too. That's why it's so important to say things that make people feel better, not worse.

Your words can help people . . . or not. Make certain that you're the kind of person who says helpful things, not hurtful things. And, make sure that you're the kind of person who helps other people feel better about themselves, not worse.

TODAY'S PRAYER

Dear Lord, I hope that the things I say can be helpful to my friends and family. Every day, I will try my best to find words that are loving and kind. Amen

DAY 260

GOD CAN HANDLE IT

Now the God of all grace, who called you to His eternal glory in Christ Jesus, will personally restore, establish, strengthen, and support you.

1 Peter 5:10 HCSB

It's a promise that is made over and over again in the Bible: whatever "it" is, God can handle it.

Life isn't always easy. Far from it! Sometimes, life can be hard, but even then, we're protected by a loving Heavenly Father. When we're worried, God can help us; when we're sad, God can comfort us. God is not just near, He is here. So we should always lift our thoughts and prayers to Him. When we do, He will answer our prayers. Why? Because He is our Shepherd, and He has promised to protect us now and forever.

TODAY'S PRAYER

Dear Lord, it's easy to talk about putting You first, but it's harder to do it in real life. Please help me put You first-really first-and not just talk about it. Amen

DAY 261

Happy Thoughts

Those who are pure in their thinking are happy, because they will be with God.

Matthew 5:8 NCV

Thoughts have the power to lift our spirits, to improve our lives, and to strengthen our relationship with God. But, our thoughts also have the power to hurt us if we focus too much on things that put distance between us and God.

Today, make your thoughts an offering to God. Seek-by the things you think and the actions you take-to honor Him and serve Him. He deserves no less. And neither, for that matter, do you.

A TIP TO START YOUR DAY

It is important to guide your thoughts to the happy side of life, not the unhappy side.

TODAY'S PRAYER

Dear Lord, I remember You are my Teacher.
Help me to learn from You. And then,
let me show others what it means to be
a kind, generous, loving Christian. Amen

Finish What You Begin

We say they are happy because they did not give up. You have heard about Job's patience, and you know the Lord's purpose for him in the end. You know the Lord is full of mercy and is kind.

James 5:11 NCV

Jesus finished what He began, and so should you. Jesus didn't give in, and neither should you. Jesus did what was right, and so should you.

Are you facing something that is hard for you to do? If so, you may be tempted to quit. If so, remember this: whatever your problem, God can handle it. Your job is to keep working until He does.

A TIP TO START YOUR DAY

If things don't work out at first, don't quit. If you never try, you'll never know how good you can be.

TODAY'S PRAYER

Dear Lord, sometimes it can be easy to quit and hard to keep going. Tomorrow and every day after that, help me finish the work that You want me to do. Amen

DAY 263

Very Big ideas about your Prayers

To start your day, take a few minutes to talk to your mom or dad about what these two quotations mean.

Prayer accomplishes more than anything else.

Bill Bright

Take life one day and one prayer at a time.

Stormie Omartian

TODAY'S PRAYER

Dear God, You have given me the gift of eternal life through Christ Jesus. I thank You for that gift, and I will try hard to be the kind of person who shows other people what it means to be a good Christian. Amen

DAY 264

GOOD THINGS HAPPEN WHEN YOU SHARE

Be generous to the poor—you'll never go hungry; shut your eyes to their needs, and run a gauntlet of curses.

Proverbs 28:27 MSG

The more you share, the quicker you'll discover this fact: Good things happen to people (like you) who are kind enough to share the blessings that God has given them.

Sharing makes you feel better about yourself. Whether you're at home or at school, remember that the best rewards go to the kids who are kind and generous—not to the people who are unkind or stingy. So do what's right: share. You'll feel lots better about yourself when you do.

TODAY'S PRAYER

Dear Lord, I can't really enjoy my blessings until I share them. Let me learn to be a generous person, and let me say "thanks" to You by sharing some of the gifts that You have already given me. Amen

DAY 265

You Can Do Big Things

Success, success to you, and success to those who help you, for your God will help you . . . .

1 Chronicles 12:18 NIV

God makes this promise: If you have faith in Him, you can do BIG things! So if you have something important to do, pray about it and ask God for help. When you ask God to help you, He will. And while you're at it, never be afraid to ask your parents for help.

When you talk things over with your parents, you'll soon discover that they want you to do BIG things . . . and they can give you LOTS of help.

A VERY VEGGIE BRIGHT IDEA

Success and happiness are not destinations. They are exciting, never-ending journeys.

Zig Ziglar

TODAY'S PRAYER

Dear Lord, You have given me a wonderful gift: time here on earth. Let me use it wisely every day that I live. Amen

DAY 266

Don't Give Up! Be Hopeful

We have this hope—like a sure and firm anchor of the soul—
that enters the inner sanctuary behind the curtain.

Hebrews 6:19 HCSB

A re you a hope-filled boy? Hopefully so!
When you stop to think about it, you have lots of reasons to be hopeful: God loves you, your family loves you, and you've got a very bright future ahead of you. So trust God, and be hopeful. When you do, you'll be a happier person . . . and God will smile.

A TIP TO START YOUR DAY

As long as God is in His heaven, there's always hope . . . so don't give up!

TODAY'S PRAYER

Dear God, help me remember to keep hope in my heart . . . and praise on my lips for You! Amen

DAY 267

Spend Time with God Every Day

Careful planning puts you ahead in the long run; hurry and scurry puts you further behind.

Proverbs 21:5 MSG

How much time do you spend getting to know God? A lot? A little? Almost none? Hopefully, you answered "a lot."

God loved this world so much that He sent His Son to save it. And now only one real question remains for you: What will you do in response to God's love? God deserves your prayers, your obedience, and your love–and He deserves these things all day every day, not just on Sunday mornings.

A TIP TO START YOUR DAY

You should plan to spend some time with God every day . . . and you should stick to your plan!

TODAY'S PRAYER

Dear Lord, I have lots of things to do, but nothing I do is more important than the time I spend with You. I thank You, Lord, for Your blessings, for Your Son, and for Your Bible. I will take time to read it every day. Amen

Life is a Gift

Live full lives, full in the fullness of God. God can do anything, you know—far more than you could ever imagine or guess or request in your wildest dreams! He does it not by pushing us around but by working within us, his Spirit deeply and gently within us.

Ephesians 3:19-20 MSG

Life is a gift from God. A wonderful gift; a glorious gift; an amazing gift. Your job is to unwrap that gift, to use it wisely, and to give thanks to the Giver.

Are you going to treat this day (and every one hereafter) as a special gift to be enjoyed and celebrated? You should—and if you really want to please God, that's exactly what you will do.

A VERY VEGGIE BRIGHT IDEA

Life is a glorious opportunity.

Billy Graham

TODAY'S PRAYER

Dear Lord, help me become a boy who always lets Your Spirit live and grow in my heart. Amen

TRY TO MEMORIZE THIS VERSE

"For I know the plans I have for you,"
declares the LORD,
"plans to prosper you and
not to harm you,
plans to give you hope and a future."
Jeremiah 29:11 NIV

This is an important Bible verse. Practice saying it several times. And then, talk to your mom or dad about exactly what the verse means . . .

A TIP FOR PARENTS
Today, talk to your child about . . . God's plan.

TODAY'S PRAYER
Dear Lord, You made me, and You made me for a reason. Help me to follow Your commandments and follow Your plan, now and always. Amen

GOD LOVES YOU . . .
ALWAYS TRUST HIM

"I say this because I know what I am planning for you,"
says the Lord. "I have good plans for you, not plans to hurt
you. I will give you hope and a good future."

Jeremiah 29:11 NCV

Sometimes, things happen that we simply don't understand. And that's exactly how God intends it! You see God has given us many gifts, but He hasn't given us the power to understand everything that happens in our world (that comes later, when we get to heaven!).

The Bible tells us God's plans are far bigger than we humans can possibly understand. That's one of the reasons that God doesn't make His plans clear to us. But even when we can't understand why God allows certain things to happen, we can trust His love for us.

The Bible does make one part of God's plan perfectly clear: we should accept His Son Jesus into our hearts so that we might have eternal life (John 3:16). And when we do, we are protected today and forever.

TODAY'S PRAYER

Dear Lord, Your plans are perfect. I will do my best to follow Your plans and to obey Your commandments. Amen

Honesty Pays

Therefore, whatever you want others to do for you, do also the same for them–this is the Law and the Prophets.

Matthew 7:12 HCSB

D o you want other people to be honest with you? Of course you do. And that's why you should be honest with them. The words of Matthew 7:12 remind us that, as believers in Christ, we should treat others as we wish to be treated. And that means telling them the truth!

The Golden Rule is your tool for deciding how you will treat other people. When you use the Golden Rule as your guide for living, your words and your actions will be pleasing to other people and to God.

TODAY'S PRAYER

Dear Lord, sometimes it's hard to treat people in the same way that I want to be treated. But even when it's hard, I want to obey the Golden Rule now and always. Amen

THINK ABOUT WHAT'S RIGHT

Keep your eyes focused on what is right. Keep looking straight ahead to what is good.

Proverbs 4:25 ICB

In the Book of Proverbs, King Solomon gave us wonderful advice for living wisely. Solomon said that we should keep our eyes "focused on what is right." In other words, we should do our best to say and do the things that we know are pleasing to God.

The next time you're tempted to say an unkind word or to say something that isn't true, remember the advice of King Solomon. Solomon knew that it's always better to do the right thing, even when it's tempting to do otherwise. So if you know something is wrong, don't do it; instead, do what you know to be right. When you do, you'll be saving yourself a lot of trouble and you'll be obeying the Word of God.

TODAY'S PRAYER

Heavenly Father, the Bible instructs me to do what is right. So, Lord, help me understand what's right . . . and help me do it. Amen

DAY 273

THE KID IN THE MIRROR

For you made us only a little lower than God, and you crowned us with glory and honor.

Psalm 8:5 NLT

Do you like the boy you see when you look into the mirror? You should! After all, the person in the mirror is a very special person who is made—and loved—by God.

In fact, you are loved in many, many ways: God loves you, your parents love you, and your family loves you, for starters. So you should love yourself, too.

So here's something to think about: since God thinks you're special, and since so many people think you're special, isn't it about time for you to agree with them? Of course it is! It's time to say, "You're very wonderful and very special," to the person you see in the mirror.

TODAY'S PRAYER

Dear Lord, thank You for Your Son. Because Jesus loves me, I will feel good about myself, my family, and my future. Amen

DAY 274

TRY TO MEMORIZE THIS VERSE

*Good people's words
will help many others.*

Proverbs 10:21 NCV

*This is an important Bible verse. Practice saying it
several times. And then, talk to your mom or dad
about exactly what the verse means . . .*

A TIP FOR PARENTS

Today, talk to your child about . . . helping others.

TODAY'S PRAYER

Dear Lord, I want to be helpful and kind. Give me a loving
heart, Lord, and help me find ways to help people
in need. Amen

OBEDIENCE AND HAPPINESS GO TOGETHER

You are young, but do not let anyone treat you as if you were not important. Be an example to show the believers how they should live. Show them with your words, with the way you live, with your love, with your faith, and with your pure life.

1 Timothy 4:12 ICB

Do you want to be happy? Then you should learn to obey your parents and your teachers. And, of course, you should also learn to obey God. When you do, you'll discover that happiness goes hand-in-hand with good behavior.

The happiest people do not misbehave; the happiest people are not cruel or greedy. The happiest people don't disobey their parents, their teachers, or their Father in heaven. The happiest people are those who obey the rules . . .

TODAY'S PRAYER

Dear Lord, Your laws are right for me; let me live by those laws. And, let me be a good example for others so that they, too, might follow in the footsteps of Your Son, Jesus. Amen

DAY 276

WHEN BAD THINGS HAPPEN

I leave you peace; my peace I give you. I do not give it to you as the world does. So don't let your hearts be troubled or afraid.

John 14:27 NCV

When bad things happen, it's understandable that we might feel afraid. In fact, it's good to be afraid if our fears keep us from behaving foolishly (by the way, if that little voice inside your head tells you that doing something is dangerous, don't do it).

When our own troubles—or the world's troubles—leave us fearful, we should discuss our concerns with the people who love and care for us. Parents and grandparents can help us understand our fears, and they can help us feel better. That's why we need to talk with them.

It's okay to be afraid—all of us are fearful from time to time. And it's good to know that we can talk about our fears with loved ones and with God. When we do, we'll discover that fear lasts for a little while, but love lasts forever.

TODAY'S PRAYER

Dear Lord, when bad things happen, help me remember that You're still in charge of the whole world . . . and that you're in charge of my world, too. Amen

DAY 277

FOLLOW JESUS

"Follow Me," Jesus told them, "and I will make you into fishers of men!" Immediately they left their nets and followed Him.

Mark 1:17-18 HCSB

Who are you going to follow? Do yourself a favor—follow Jesus!

God's Word promises that when you follow in Christ's footsteps, you will learn how to behave yourself, and you'll learn how to live a good life. Jesus wants you to be a "new creation" through Him. And that's exactly what you should want for yourself, too. So talk with Jesus (through prayer) and walk with Him (by obeying His rules) now and forever.

A TIP TO START YOUR DAY

If you want to be a disciple of Christ, follow in His footsteps, obey His commandments, talk with Him often, tell others about Him, and share His never-ending love.

TODAY'S PRAYER

Dear Lord, I want to follow Jesus every day of my life. Help me to become more like Him, and help me to share His message with my family and friends. Amen

Very Big Ideas About Respecting Your Parents

To start your day, take a few minutes to talk to your mom or dad about what these two quotations mean.

The child who does not learn to obey his parents is not likely to grow up obeying any authority.

Warren Wiersbe

How wonderful it is when parents and children respect each other . . . and show it.

Jim Gallery

TODAY'S PRAYER

Dear Lord, because I want to please You, I will do my best to love everybody . . . including myself. Amen

Praise The Lord Every Day

Praise the LORD. Give thanks to the LORD, for he is good; his love endures forever.

Psalm 106:1 NIV

I f you're like most boys, you're very busy doing things and learning things. But no matter how busy you are—even if you hardly have a moment to spare—you should still slow down and say "thank You" to God!

God has given you many things, and you owe Him everything, including a GREAT BIG THANK YOU, starting now (and ending never!).

A TIP TO START YOUR DAY

Whether it's daytime or nighttime, it's always the right time to praise God.

TODAY'S PRAYER

Dear Lord, I thank You for all Your blessings, and I will praise You today, tomorrow, and every day of my life. Amen

DAY 280

Friends You Can Trust

Friends come and friends go, but a true friend sticks by you like family.

Proverbs 18:24 MSG

Real friendships are built upon both honesty and trust. As Christians, we should always try to be trustworthy friends. And, we should be thankful for the people who are loyal friends to us. When we treat other people with honesty and respect, we not only make more friends, but we also keep the friendships we've already made.

Do you want friends you can trust? Then start by being a friend they can trust. That's the way to make your friendships strong, stronger, and strongest!

A TIP TO START YOUR DAY

You make friends by being a friend. And when you choose your friends, choose wisely.

TODAY'S PRAYER

Dear Lord, thank You for good friends I can trust. Let me be a trustworthy person, Lord. And, let me be a good Christian as I follow in the footsteps of Your Son. Amen

DAY 281

WHEN TO STOP TEMPER TANTRUMS

A hot-tempered person starts fights and gets into all kinds of sin.

Proverbs 29:22 NLT

Temper tantrums are one of the silliest ways to lose self-control. Why? Because when we lose our temper, we say things that we shouldn't say, and we do things that we shouldn't do. And to make matters worse, once the tantrum is over, we usually feel embarrassed or worse.

The Bible tells us that it isn't very smart to become angry. That's why we should learn to stop temper tantrums before they get started.

TODAY'S PRAYER

Dear Lord, help me to behave myself like a good Christian! Let me keep Christ in my heart, and let me put the devil in his place: far away from me! Amen

DAY 282

GOD KNOWS YOUR SECRETS

The eyes of the Lord are in every place, keeping watch . . .

Proverbs 15:3 NKJV

Even when nobody else is watching, God is. Nothing that we say or do escapes the watchful eye of our Lord. God understands that we are not perfect, but He also wants us to live according to His rules, not our own.

The next time that you're tempted to say something that you shouldn't say or to do something that you shouldn't do, remember that you can't keep secrets from God. So don't even try!

A TIP TO START YOUR DAY

Having trouble hearing God? If so, slow yourself down, tune out the distractions, and listen carefully. God has important things to say; your task is to be still and listen.

TODAY'S PRAYER

Dear Lord, I know that You are everywhere and that You are always with me. Today and every day, I will thank You, Father, for Your protection and for Your love. Amen

DAY 283

TRY TO MEMORIZE THIS VERSE

*Everything is possible
to the one who believes.*

Mark 9:23 HCSB

*This is an important Bible verse about faith.
Practice saying it several times. And then,
talk to your mom or dad about exactly
what the verse means . . .*

A TIP FOR PARENTS
Today, talk to your child about . . .
the importance of faith.

TODAY'S PRAYER
Dear God, when I have faith, I can do big things. Help
me have faith in myself, faith in my family, faith in my
future, and faith in You. Amen

DAY 284

A HELPING HAND

Hatred stirs up trouble, but love forgives all wrongs.

Proverbs 10:12 NCV

Sometimes, young people can be thoughtless, or even cruel. Some kids make fun of other people, and when they do so, it's wrong. Period.

As Christians, we should be kind to everyone. And, if other kids say unkind things to a child or make fun of him or her, it's up to us to step in and lend a helping hand.

So, be a boy who is known for your kindness, not for your cruelty. That's how God wants you to behave. Period.

TODAY'S PRAYER

Dear Lord, if other people are cruel, I know that I should never join in. So even if my friends behave badly, I'll do what's right. Help me do the right thing, Lord, tomorrow and every day after that. Amen

iT's GooD To SHaRe

It is well with the man who deals generously and lends.

Psalm 112:5 RSV

t's a fact: sharing makes you a better person. Why? Because when you share, you're doing several things: first, you're obeying God; and you're making your corner of the world a better place; and you're learning exactly what it feels like to be a generous, loving person.

When you share, you have the fun of knowing that your good deeds are making other people happy. When you share, you're learning how to become a better person. When you share, you're making things better for other people and for yourself. So do the right thing: share!

A VERY VEGGIE BRIGHT IDEA

Find out how much God has given you and from it take what you need; the remainder is needed by others.

St. Augustine

TODAY'S PRAYER

Dear Lord, it's easy to share with some people and difficult to share with others. Let me be kind to all people so that I might follow in the footsteps of Your Son. Amen

iT Pays To Be PaTieNT

Knowing God leads to self-control. Self-control leads to patient endurance, and patient endurance leads to godliness.

2 Peter 1:6 NLT

Sometimes it's hard to sit still, and sometimes it's even harder to be patient! So here's something worth remembering: God wants us to be patient, and we must obey Him or suffer the consequences.

We should be patient with our families, with our friends, and with ourselves . . . especially with ourselves.

A TIP TO START YOUR DAY

If you think you're about to say or do something you'll regret later, slow down and take a deep breath, or two deep breaths, or ten, or . . . well you get the idea.

TODAY'S PRAYER

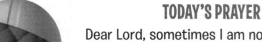

Dear Lord, sometimes I am not very patient. Slow me down and calm me down. Help me to think wisely and to act wisely. Now and always, help me to learn the wisdom of patience. Amen

DAY 287

VERY BIG IDEAS ABOUT PLEASING GOD

To start your day, take a few minutes to talk to your mom or dad about what these two quotations mean.

Make God's will the focus of your life day by day. If you seek to please Him and Him alone, you'll find yourself satisfied with life.

Kay Arthur

You must never sacrifice your relationship with God for the sake of a relationship with another person.

Charles Stanley

TODAY'S PRAYER

Dear Lord, You have given me so much. Today and every day I will do my best to please You by thinking good thoughts and doing good deeds. Amen

DAY 288

You'll Earn Big Rewards When You Do the Right Thing

Do you want to be counted wise, to build a reputation for wisdom? Here's what you do: Live well, live wisely, live humbly. It's the way you live, not the way you talk, that counts.

James 3:13 MSG

If you open up a dictionary, you'll see that the word "wisdom" means "using good judgment, and knowing what is true." But there's more to it than that. It's not enough to know what's right—if you want to be wise, you must also do what's right.

The Bible promises that when you do smart things, you'll earn big rewards, so slow down and think about things before you do them, not after.

TODAY'S PRAYER

Dear Lord, let me be patient with other people's mistakes. And let me be patient with my own. I know that I still have so many things to learn. I won't stop learning, I won't give up, and I won't stop growing up. Every day, I will do my best to become a little bit more like the person You intend for me to be. Amen

DAY 289

Learn to Control Your Temper

And be careful that when you get on each other's nerves you don't snap at each other. Look for the best in each other, and always do your best to bring it out.

1 Thessalonians 5:15 MSG

The Bible tells us that we should control our tempers. But sometimes, especially when we're angry or frustrated, our words and our actions may not be so gentle. Sometimes, we may say things or do things that are unkind or hurtful to others. When we do, we're wrong.

The next time you're tempted to strike out in anger, don't. And if you want to help your family and friends, remember that kind words are the kind of words you should speak. Always!

TODAY'S PRAYER

Dear Lord, when I become angry, help me to remember that You offer me peace and patience. I'll look to You, God, for wisdom, for patience, and for the peace that only You can give. Amen

DAY 290

ANGER CAUSES TROUBLE

Patience is better than strength.

Proverbs 16:32 ICB

I n the Book of Proverbs, King Solomon gave us wonderful advice for living wisely. Solomon warned that impatience and anger lead only to trouble. And he was right!

The next time you're tempted to say an unkind word or to throw a temper tantrum, remember Solomon. He was one of the wisest men who ever lived, and he knew that it's always better to be patient. So remain calm and remember that patience is best. After all, if it's good enough for a wise man like Solomon, it should be good enough for us, too.

TODAY'S PRAYER

Dear Lord, give me a heart that is filled with love, patience, and concern for others. Slow me down and calm me down so that I can see the needs of other people. And then, give me a loving heart so that I will do something about the needs that I see. Amen

DAY 291

PLEASING GOD IS MUCH MORE IMPORTANT THAN PLEASING FRIENDS

For am I now trying to win the favor of people, or God? Or am I striving to please people? If I were still trying to please people, I would not be a slave of Christ.

Galatians 1:10 HCSB

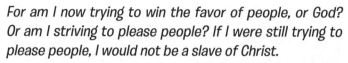

Are you a people-pleaser or a God-pleaser? Hopefully, you're far more concerned with pleasing God than you are with pleasing your friends. But face facts: even if you're a devoted Christian, you're still going to feel the urge to impress your friends–and sometimes that urge will be strong.

Here's your choice: you can choose to please God first, or you can fall victim to peer pressure. The choice is yours–and so are the consequences.

TODAY'S PRAYER

Dear Lord, help me remember that I don't have to please everybody . . . but that I should always try to please You! Amen

HOW TO TREAT OTHERS

See that no one pays back evil for evil, but always try to do good to each other and to everyone else.

1 Thessalonians 5:15 TLB

Would you like to make the world a better place? If so, you can start by practicing the Golden Rule.

Jesus said, "Whatever you want others to do for you, do also the same for them" (Matthew 7:12 HCSB). That means that you should treat other people in the very same way that you want to be treated. That's the Golden Rule.

So here's what you should do: if you want to know how to treat somebody, ask the person you see every time you look into the mirror. The answer you receive will tell you exactly what to do.

TODAY'S PRAYER

Dear Lord, help me always to do my very best to treat others as I wish to be treated. The Golden Rule is Your rule, Father; let me also make it mine. Amen

DAY 293

IT'S IMPORTANT TO OBEY YOUR PARENTS

We must obey God rather than men.

Acts 5:29 NASB

When your parents ask you to do something, do you usually obey them or do you usually ignore them? When your parents try to get your attention, do you listen or not? When your parents make rules, do you obey those rules or do you break them? Hopefully, you've learned to listen to your parents and to obey.

In order to be an obedient boy, you must first learn how to control yourself—otherwise, you won't be able to behave yourself even if you want to. Controlling yourself means that you must slow down long enough to listen to your parents, and then you must be willing to do something about the things your parents tell you to do.

When you learn the importance of obedience, you'll soon discover that good things happen when you behave yourself. And the sooner you learn to listen and to obey, the sooner those good things will start happening.

TODAY'S PRAYER

Dear Heavenly Father, when I obey, I'm a much happier person. Help me learn the importance of obeying my parents and the importance of obeying You. Amen

iF You Think, You're Right

*Though a righteous man falls seven times, he will get up,
but the wicked will stumble into ruin.*

Proverbs 24:16 HCSB

If you think you can do something, then you can probably do it. If you think you can't do something, then you
probably won't do it.

So remember this: if you're having a little trouble getting something done, don't get mad, don't get frustrated,
don't get discouraged, and don't give up. Just keep trying
. . . and believe in yourself.

When you try hard–and keep trying hard–you can really do amazing things . . . but if you quit at the first sign
of trouble, you'll miss out. So here's a good rule to follow:
when you have something that you want to finish, finish it
. . . and finish it sooner rather than later.

TODAY'S PRAYER

Dear Lord, sometimes I feel like giving up. When I
feel that way, help me do the right thing . . . and
help me finish the work You want me to do. Amen

DAY 295

Very Big ideas about Serving Other People

To start your day, take a few minutes to talk to your mom or dad about what these two quotations mean.

There are times when we are called to love, expecting nothing in return.
There are times when we are called to give money to people who will never say thanks, to forgive those who won't forgive us, to come early and stay late when no one else notices.

Max Lucado

God will open up places of service for you as He sees you are ready. Meanwhile, study the Bible and give yourself a chance to grow.

Warren Wiersbe

TODAY'S PRAYER

Father, let my life be a life of service. You have given me so many opportunities to serve. Let me recognize those opportunities and use them to serve Your kingdom. Amen

DAY 296

Pray for Everybody

Hatred stirs up trouble, but love forgives all wrongs.

Proverbs 10:12 NCV

I t's usually pretty easy to pray for your friends and family members—all you have to do is find the time. But when it comes to praying for people who have hurt you, well that's a different matter entirely!

Like it or not, God says that you've got to pray for the folks you like and for the folks you don't like. Why? Well maybe it's because God knows that He has already forgiven you, and now He thinks it's about time for you to forgive them.

A TIP TO START YOUR DAY

Martin Luther said, "If I should neglect prayer but a single day, I should lose a great deal of the fire of faith." Those words apply to you, too.

TODAY'S PRAYER

Dear Lord, when I forgive other people, I know that I am doing what's right. So give me a forgiving heart, Lord, this day and every day. Amen

DAY 297

Laugh Whenever You Can

A joyful heart is good medicine . . .

Proverbs 17:22 HCSB

God doesn't want us to spend our lives moping around with frowns on our faces. Far from it! God tells us that a happy heart is a very good thing to have.

So if you're afraid to laugh out loud, don't be. Remember that God wouldn't have given you the gift of laughter if He hadn't intended for you to use it. And remember: if you're laughing, that does not mean that you're unconcerned about people who may be hurting. It simply means that you've taken a little time to have fun, and that's good because God wants you to have a joyful heart.

A VERY VEGGIE BRIGHT IDEA

Laughter is God's medicine. Everybody ought to bathe in it.

Henry Ward Beecher

TODAY'S PRAYER

Dear Lord, You have given me a priceless gift: the gift of life. I will give thanks for that gift and enjoy it. Amen

WHEN YOU MAKE A MISTAKE, GOD WILL FORGIVE YOU

If we claim that we're free of sin, we're only fooling ourselves. A claim like that is errant nonsense. On the other hand, if we admit our sins–make a clean breast of them–he won't let us down; he'll be true to himself. He'll forgive our sins and purge us of all wrongdoing.

1 John 1:8-9 MSG

Are you perfect? Of course not! Even if you're a very good boy, you're bound to mistakes.

When you make a mistake, you must try your best to learn from it (so that you won't make the very same mistake again). And, if you have hurt someone–or if you have disobeyed God–you must ask for forgiveness. And here's the good news: when you ask for God's forgiveness, He will always give it. God forgives you every single time you ask Him to. So ask!

TODAY'S PRAYER

Dear Lord, You forgive me for my mistakes. Thank You, Father. I will try hard to forgive other people, just like You have forgiven me. Amen

DAY 299

TELLING THE TRUTH IS THE RIGHT THING TO DO

Tell each other the truth because we all belong to each other...

Ephesians 4:25 ICB

It's important to be honest. When you tell the truth, you'll feel better about yourself, and other people will feel better about you, too. But that's not all. When you tell the truth, God knows–and He will reward you for your honesty.

Telling the truth is hard sometimes. But it's better to be honest, even when it's hard. So remember this: telling the truth is always the right thing to do . . . always.

TODAY'S PRAYER

Dear Lord, I know that You want me to be an honest person. Help me to be honest and obedient to You this day and every day of my life. Amen

DAY 300

FORGIVE OTHER PEOPLE'S MISTAKES

I will instruct you and teach you in the way you should go;
I will counsel you and watch over you.

Psalm 32:8 NIV

When other people make mistakes, you must find a way to forgive them. And when you make mistakes, as you will from time to time, you must hope that other people will forgive you, too.

When you have done things that you regret, you should apologize, you should clean up the mess you've made, you should learn from your mistakes, and–last but not least–you should forgive yourself. Mistakes happen . . . it's simply a fact of life, and it's simply a part of growing up. So don't be too hard on yourself, especially if you've learned something along the way.

A VERY VEGGIE BRIGHT IDEA

Father, take our mistakes and turn them into opportunities.

Max Lucado

TODAY'S PRAYER

Dear Lord, sometimes I make mistakes, and when I do, please help me learn from them. Amen

DAY 301

in His Footsteps

Whoever serves me must follow me. Then my servant will be with me everywhere I am. My Father will honor anyone who serves me.

John 12:26 NCV

Jesus walks with you. Are you walking with Him? Hopefully, you will choose to walk with Him today, tomorrow, and every day of your life.

Jesus has called upon believers of every generation (and that includes you) to follow in His footsteps. Will you follow? Please answer that question with a GREAT BIG YES. When you do, your heart will be filled with a GREAT BIG LOVE for Him!

A TIP TO START YOUR DAY

If you're really following Christ, you'll never stay lost for long.

TODAY'S PRAYER

Dear Lord, today and every day I want to follow Jesus. Help me to think the right thoughts and do the right things now and always. Amen

DAY 302

Lessons You Can Learn

Remember what you are taught. And listen carefully to words of knowledge.

Proverbs 23:12 ICB

You can learn a lot about life by paying attention to the things that happen around you . . . and that's exactly what God wants you to do. God is trying to teach you things, and you can learn those things the easy way (by paying attention and obeying God's rules) or the hard way (by making the same mistakes over and over again until you finally learn something from them). Of course, it's better to learn things sooner rather than later . . . starting now.

A VERY VEGGIE BRIGHT IDEA

While it is wise to learn from experience, it is wiser to learn from the experience of others.

Rick Warren

TODAY'S PRAYER

Dear Lord, I have so much to learn. Help me keep my eyes open wide. And, help me learn the lessons You want me to learn. Amen

DAY 303

Very Big ideas about Prayer

To start your day, take a few minutes to talk to your mom or dad about what these two quotations mean.

Just as our faith strengthens our prayer life, so do our prayers deepen our faith. Let us pray often, starting today, for a deeper, more powerful faith.

Shirley Dobson

Don't be overwhelmed . . . take it one day and one prayer at a time.

Stormie Omartian

TODAY'S PRAYER

Dear Lord, tomorrow and every day after that, I will talk with You as often as I can, and I will do my best to follow in the footsteps of Your Son. Amen

DAY 304

ALWAYS GROWING

When I was a child, I spoke like a child, I thought like a child, I reasoned like a child. When I became a man, I put aside childish things.

1 Corinthians 13:11 HCSB

You're growing up day by day, and it's a wonderful thing to watch. Every day, you're learning new things and doing new things. Good for you!

And when should you stop growing up? Hopefully never! That way, you'll always be learning more and doing more.

Do you think it's good to keep growing and growing and growing? If you said "yes," you're right. So remember: you're a very special person today . . . and you'll be just as special when you've grown a little bit more tomorrow.

A TIP TO START YOUR DAY

Grown-ups still have plenty to learn . . . and so do you!

TODAY'S PRAYER

Dear Lord, thank You for letting me grow a little bit more every day. I thank You for the person I am . . . and for the person I can become. Amen

Happiness and Honesty Go Together

Lead a quiet and peaceable life in all godliness and honesty.

1 Timothy 2:2 KJV

Have you ever said something that wasn't true? When you did, were you sorry for what you had said? Probably so.

When we're dishonest, we make ourselves unhappy in surprising ways. Here are just a few troubles that result from dishonesty: we feel guilty, and we are usually found out, and we disappoint others and we disappoint God. It's easy to see that lies always cause more problems than they solve.

Happiness and honesty always go hand in hand. But it's up to you to make sure that you go hand in hand with them!

TODAY'S PRAYER

Dear Lord, let me always tell the truth, even when it's hard. Amen

DAY 306

Having Trouble Behaving Yourself? Pray About It!

Rejoice always! Pray constantly. Give thanks in everything, for this is God's will for you in Christ Jesus.

1 Thessalonians 5:16-18 HCSB

Would you like to become a more obedient boy? Then pray about it. Would you like to learn how to behave yourself a little bit better? Then pray about it. Want to be able to think about things before you get into trouble, not after? Pray for God's help.

If you have questions about whether you should do something or not, pray about it. If there is something you're worried about, ask God to comfort you. And as you pray more, you'll discover that God is always near and that He's always ready to hear from you. So don't worry about things; pray about them. God is waiting to hear from you . . . so what are you waiting for?

TODAY'S PRAYER

Dear Lord, when I pray often, things go better for me. So, I will talk with You as often as I can, and I will thank You for all the wonderful things You do. Amen

DAY 307

Questions?

An indecisive man is unstable in all his ways.

James 1:8 HCSB

God doesn't explain Himself in ways that we humans would prefer. When innocent people are hurt, we question God because we can't figure out exactly what He's doing, or why. But even when we can't answer tough questions like these, we must trust in God's love, God's wisdom, and God's plan.

And while we're waiting for that wonderful day when all our questions will be answered (in heaven), we should use the time that we have here on earth to help the people who need it most.

TODAY'S PRAYER

Dear Lord, while I am growing up, I still have so many things to learn. Let me remember that the most important lessons are the ones that I learn every day from my parents and from You. Amen

DAY 308

GOD'S ANGELS ARE REAL . . . AND THEY'RE NEAR

Don't neglect to show hospitality, for by doing this some have welcomed angels as guests without knowing it.

Hebrews 13:2 HCSB

The Bible has a lot to say about angels. But maybe you've wondered if angels are really real. If so, wonder no more! If the Bible tells you something, you can be sure that it's true.

The Bible teaches us that angels come from God, so that means they are good and they are helpful. So we don't need to fear angels . . . but neither do we need to pretend that they don't exist!

A VERY VEGGIE BRIGHT IDEA

I believe in angels because the Bible says there are angels; and I believe the Bible to be the true Word of God.

Billy Graham

TODAY'S PRAYER

Dear Lord, I thank You for Your angels. And, I thank You for all the ways You protect me this day and every day. Amen

Honesty is always The Right Policy

Therefore laying aside falsehood, speak truth, each one of you, with his neighbor, for we are members of one another.

Ephesians 4:25 NASB

Sometimes people lie, and sometimes they get away with it. But that doesn't mean that it's wise to lie. And that doesn't make lying the right thing to do. Far from it.

Whatever the problem, lying is always a bad solution. And, besides, lying is always against the will of God. So even if other people lie, don't ever believe that they have lied successfully. There's no such thing as a successful lie.

A VERY VEGGIE BRIGHT IDEA

When you talk, choose the very same words that you would use if Jesus were looking over your shoulder. Because He is.

Marie T. Freeman

TODAY'S PRAYER

Dear Lord, help me tell the truth every day of my life. Amen

DAY 310

EVERYBODY NEEDS TO HEAR KIND WORDS

Avoid irreverent, empty speech, for this will produce an even greater measure of godlessness.

2 Timothy 2:16 HCSB

Your words can help other people . . . or not. So please make sure that you're the kind of guy who says helpful things, not hurtful things. You'll feel better about yourself when you help other people feel better about themselves.

Do you like for people to say kind words to you? Of course you do! And that's exactly how other people feel, too. That's why it's so important to say things that make people feel better, not worse.

Everybody needs to hear kind words, and that's exactly the kind of words they should hear from you!

TODAY'S PRAYER

Dear Lord, the Bible teaches me that You hear every word I say. So, I will do my best to say things that are kind, honest, and worthy of Your Son. Amen

DAY 311

Give Thanks For the Memories

I give thanks to my God for every remembrance of you.

Philippians 1:3 HCSB

In his letter to the Philippians, Paul wrote to his distant friends saying that he thanked God every time he remembered them. We, too, should thank God for the family and friends He has brought into our lives.

Today, let's give thanks to God for all the people who love us, for brothers and sisters, parents and grandparents, aunts and uncles, cousins and friends. And then, as a way of thanking God, let's obey Him by being especially kind to our loved ones. They deserve it, and so does He.

A VERY VEGGIE BRIGHT IDEA

The best times in life are made a thousand times better when shared with a dear friend.

Luci Swindoll

TODAY'S PRAYER

Lord, thank You for my good friends. Let me be a good friend to others, and let my love for Jesus guide my friendships now and always. Amen

DAY 312

WHen You'Re Sad

Those people who know they have great spiritual needs are happy, because the kingdom of heaven belongs to them. Those who are sad now are happy, because God will comfort them.

Matthew 5:3-4 NCV

Sometimes, you feel happy, and sometimes you don't. When you're feeling sad, here are two very important things you should do: 1. Talk to your parents about your feelings. 2. Talk to God about your feelings.

Talking with your parents is helpful because your mom and dad understand this: the problems that seem VERY BIG to you today probably won't seem so big tomorrow.

Talking with God helps because God hears your prayers and He helps make things better.

So the next time you're sad, don't hold your feelings inside–talk things over with your parents and with God. When you do, you'll feel better . . . and so will they!

TODAY'S PRAYER

Dear Lord, when I am sad, I know that I can talk to my parents . . . and to You. Thank You, Lord, for listening to me. And thank You for parents who love me and listen to me. Amen

DAY 313

Be Willing to Help

There are different kinds of gifts, but they are all from the same Spirit. There are different ways to serve but the same Lord to serve.

1 Corinthians 12:4-5 NCV

I f we want to be Christ's servants, we must be willing to help people who can't help themselves. Jesus told the story of the "Good Samaritan," a man who helped a fellow traveler when no one else would. We, too, should be good Samaritans when we find people who need our help.

This very day, you will encounter someone who needs a word of encouragement, or a pat on the back, or a helping hand, or a heartfelt prayer. And, if you don't reach out to your friend, who will?

So today, find somebody who needs a hug or a helping hand . . . and give them both.

TODAY'S PRAYER

Dear Lord, help me to make Your world a better place. I can't fix all the world's troubles, but I can help make things better with kind words, good deeds, and sincere prayers. Let my actions and my prayers be pleasing to You, Lord, now and forever. Amen

DAY 314

TRY TO MEMORIZE THIS VERSE

Cast all your anxiety on him because he cares for you.

I Peter 5:7 NIV

This is an important Bible verse. Practice saying it several times. And then, talk to your mom or dad about exactly what the verse means . . .

A TIP FOR PARENTS

Today, talk to your child about . . . trusting God.

TODAY'S PRAYER

Dear Lord, when things happen that I don't fully understand, help me put my trust in You. Because I know that You love me, I will do my best to put my worries aside and trust You to protect me always. Amen

DAY 315

THINK GOOD THOUGHTS

Come near to God, and God will come near to you. You sinners, clean sin out of your lives. You who are trying to follow God and the world at the same time, make your thinking pure.

James 4:8 NCV

Here's something to think about: if you want to guard your heart, you must also guard your thoughts. Why? Because thoughts are very powerful, that's why.

Today, try your best to think good thoughts, happy thoughts, and helpful thoughts. When you think good thoughts, you'll be glad you did . . . and your friends and family will be glad, too.

A TIP TO START YOUR DAY

Good thoughts can lead you to some very good places . . . and bad thoughts can lead elsewhere.

TODAY'S PRAYER

Dear Lord, You teach me that my thoughts are important to You. Help me to think good thoughts and to do good deeds, today, tomorrow, and forever. Amen

DAY 316

GOD SOLVES PROBLEMS

Since God assured us, "I'll never let you down, never walk off and leave you," we can boldly quote, God is there, ready to help; I'm fearless no matter what. Who or what can get to me?

Hebrews 13:5-6 MSG

D o you have a problem that you haven't been able to solve? Welcome to the club! Life is full of problems that don't have easy solutions. But if you have a problem that you can't solve, there is something you can do: turn that problem over to God. He can handle it.

God has a way of solving our problems if we let Him; our job is to let Him. God can handle things that we can't. And the sooner we turn our concerns over to Him, the sooner He will go to work solving those troubles that are simply too big for us to handle.

If you're worried or discouraged, pray about it. And ask your parents and friends to pray about it, too. And then stop worrying because no problem is too big for God, not even yours.

TODAY'S PRAYER

Dear Lord, there's no problem that is too big for You. Thank You, Father, for protecting me today, tomorrow, and forever. Amen

DAY 317

VERY BIG IDEAS ABOUT NOT PUTTING THINGS OFF UNTIL THE LAST MINUTE

To start your day, take a few minutes to talk to your mom or dad about what these two quotations mean.

Do the unpleasant work first and enjoy the rest of the day.

Marie T. Freeman

Every time you refuse to face up to life and its problems, you weaken your character.

E. Stanley Jones

TODAY'S PRAYER

Dear Lord, You have many things You want me to do. When there are things that I need to do, let me do them quickly and well. Amen

DAY 318

Listen to God

Continue to ask, and God will give to you. Continue to search, and you will find. Continue to knock, and the door will open for you.

Matthew 7:7 ICB

God has many things He wants to tell us, and He has many ways to get His messages through to us. Sometimes, God speaks to us through the Bible, sometimes He talks to us in prayer, and sometimes He delivers His messages through the words of parents, family members, teachers, or friends.

God wants us to be loving, kind, and patient, not rude or mean! Today and every day, listen carefully to your Heavenly Father. His love lasts forever and His wisdom never fails.

TODAY'S PRAYER

Dear Lord, You're trying to tell me many things. Help me to listen carefully, Father. And let me learn. Amen

DAY 319

TRY TO MEMORIZE THIS VERSE

A cheerful heart has a continual feast.

Proverbs 15:15 HCSB

This is an important Bible verse. Practice saying it several times. And then, talk to your mom or dad about exactly what the verse means . . .

A TIP FOR PARENTS

Today, talk to your child about . . .
the benefits of a happy heart.

TODAY'S PRAYER

Dear Lord, I am thankful for all the blessings
You have given me. Let me be a happy
Christian, Father, as I share Your joy with
friends, with family, and with the world. Amen

DAY 320

LISTENING, TO DIRECTIONS

A fool's way is right in his own eyes, but whoever listens to counsel is wise.

Proverbs 12:15 HCSB

Directions, directions, directions. It seems like somebody is always giving you directions: telling you where to go, how to behave, and what to do next. But sometimes all these directions can be confusing! How can you understand everything that everybody tells you? The answer, of course, is that you must pay careful attention to those directions . . . and that means listening.

To become a careful listener, here are some things you must do: 1. Don't talk when you're supposed to be listening (your ears work best when your mouth is closed); 2. Watch the person who's giving the directions (when your eyes and ears work together, it's easier to understand things); 3. If you don't understand something, ask a question (it's better to ask now than to make a mistake later).

TODAY'S PRAYER

Dear Lord, make me a good listener, especially when I'm listening to people who have much to teach me. Amen

DAY 321

TRY TO MEMORIZE THESE VERSES

*The Lord is my shepherd;
I shall not want.
He makes me to lie down
in green pastures;
He leads me beside the still waters.
He restores my soul.*

Psalm 23:1-3 NKJV

This is an important Bible verse. Practice saying it several times. And then, talk to mom or dad about exactly what the verse means . . .

A TIP FOR PARENTS

Today, talk to your child about . . . God's protection.

TODAY'S PRAYER

Dear Lord, because You watch over us, we don't have to be afraid. Because You are with us always, we can have hope. Thank You, Lord, for protecting us today, tomorrow, and forever. Amen

DAY 322

SLOW DOWN AND CALM DOWN!

Don't let your spirit rush to be angry, for anger abides in the heart of fools.

Ecclesiastes 7:9 HCSB

When you're angry, you will be tempted to say things and do things that you'll be sorry about later. And, since you don't want to be sorry later, think before you do something! Instead of doing things in a hurry, slow down long enough to calm yourself down.

Jesus does not intend that you strike out against other people, and He doesn't intend that your heart be troubled by anger. Your heart should instead be filled with love, just like Jesus' heart was . . . and is!

TODAY'S PRAYER

Dear Lord, when I become upset, calm me down. When I'm about to throw a temper tantrum, help me control my anger. When I feel the urge to hurt other people, let me remember that Jesus forgave other folks, and I should, too. Amen

DAY 323

IT'S ALWAYS THE RIGHT TIME TO DO WHAT'S RIGHT

Be imitators of God, therefore, as dearly loved children.

Ephesians 5:1 NIV

D o you try hard to control yourself? If so, that's good because God wants all His children (including you) to behave themselves.

Sometimes, it's hard to be a well-behaved boy, especially if you have friends who don't behave nicely. But if your friends misbehave, don't imitate them. Instead, listen to your conscience, talk to your parents, and do the right thing . . . NOW!

A TIP TO START YOUR DAY

Start now! If you really want to become a well-behaved person, the best day to get started is this one.

TODAY'S PRAYER

Dear Lord, the Bible teaches me to follow Jesus, and that's what I want to do. So, Father, please help me show other people what it means to be a good person and a good Christian. Amen

DAY 324

ALWAYS OBEY THE GOLDEN RULE

Do for other people the same things you want them to do for you.

Matthew 7:12 ICB

Some rules are easier to understand than they are to live by. Jesus told us that we should treat other people in the same way that we would want to be treated: that's the Golden Rule. But sometimes, especially when we're tired or upset, that rule is very hard to follow.

Jesus wants us to treat other people with respect, kindness, courtesy, and love. When we do, we make our families and friends happy . . . and we make our Father in heaven very proud.

A VERY VEGGIE BRIGHT IDEA

The #1 rule of friendship is the Golden one.

Jim Gallery

TODAY'S PRAYER

Dear God, help me remember to treat other people the same way that I want to be treated. Help me be kind, considerate, and helpful this day and every day. Amen

DAY 325

Lies Can Lead to Trouble

Your heart must not be troubled. Believe in God; believe also in Me.

John 14:1 HCSB

When we tell a lie, trouble starts. Lots of trouble. But when we tell the truth–and nothing but the truth–we stop Old Man Trouble in his tracks.

When we always tell the truth, we make our worries smaller, not bigger. And that's precisely what God wants us to do.

So, if you'd like to have fewer worries and more happiness, abide by this simple rule: tell the truth, the whole truth, and nothing but the truth. When you do, you'll make many of your worries disappear altogether. And that's the truth!

TODAY'S PRAYER

Dear Lord, if I say something that isn't exactly true, it makes me worry. So help me tell the truth more . . . and worry less. Amen

DAY 326

VERY BIG IDEAS ABOUT FORGIVENESS

To start your day, take a few minutes to talk to your mom or dad about what these two quotations mean.

There are some facts that will never change. One fact is that you are forgiven. He sees you better than you see yourself. And that is a glorious fact of your life.

Max Lucado

It is better to forgive and forget than to resent and remember.

Barbara Johnson

TODAY'S PRAYER

Dear Lord, thank You for loving me, even when I make mistakes. You forgive me, Lord, and so do my parents. Let me learn to forgive others, so that I can treat other people in the very same way that I have been treated. Amen

DAY 327

GOD OFFERS PEACE

Keep your lives free from the love of money and be content with what you have, because God has said, "Never will I leave you; never will I forsake you."

Hebrews 13:5 NIV

Where can we find happiness? Is it a result of being wealthy or famous? Nope. Genuine peace is a gift from God to those who trust Him and follow His commandments.

If we don't find contentment in God, we will never find it anywhere else. But, if we seek Him and obey Him, we will be blessed with joyful, peaceful, meaningful lives. When God dwells at the center of our lives, peace and contentment will belong to us just as surely as we belong to God.

TODAY'S PRAYER

Dear Lord, when I welcome Jesus into my heart, and when I obey Your commandments, I will be contented. Help me to trust Your Word and follow Your Son now and forever. Amen

DAY 328

A Love That Lasts Forever

I am the good shepherd. The good shepherd lays down his life for the sheep.

John 10:11 NIV

You've probably heard the song "Jesus Loves Me." And exactly how much does He love you? He loves you so much that He gave His life so that you might live forever with Him in heaven.

How can you repay Christ's love? By accepting Him into your heart and by obeying His rules. When you do, He will love you and bless you today, tomorrow, and forever.

A VERY VEGGIE BRIGHT IDEA

Jesus is love. He never betrays us.

Catherine Marshall

TODAY'S PRAYER

Dear Lord, I thank You for Your Son, Jesus, and for His love. I will share His love with my family and friends. Amen

DAY 329

AN ATTITUDE OF KINDNESS

Finally, all of you should be of one mind, full of sympathy toward each other, loving one another with tender hearts and humble minds.

1 Peter 3:8 NLT

An attitude of kindness starts in your heart and works its way out from there.

Do you listen to your heart when it tells you to be kind to other people? Hopefully, you do. After all, lots of people in the world aren't as fortunate as you are–and some of these folks are living very near you.

Ask your parents to help you find ways to do nice things for other people. And don't forget that everybody needs love, kindness, and respect, so you should always be ready to share those things, too.

TODAY'S PRAYER

Dear Lord, the Bible teaches me that it's important to be kind. So I'll do my best to say the right things and do the right things tomorrow and every day.
Amen

DAY 330

A Pure Heart

Keep your eyes focused on what is right, and look straight ahead to what is good.

Proverbs 4:25 NCV

Where does a good attitude begin? It starts in our hearts and works its way out from there. Jesus taught us that a pure heart is a wonderful blessing. It's up to each of us to fill our hearts with love for God, love for Jesus, and love for all people. When we do, good things happen.

Sometimes, of course, we don't feel much like feeling good. Sometimes, when we're tired, or frustrated, or angry, we simply don't want to have a good attitude. On those days when we're feeling bad, it's time to calm down and rest up.

Do you want to be the best person you can be? Then you shouldn't grow tired of doing the right things or thinking the right thoughts.

TODAY'S PRAYER

Dear Lord, let me have an attitude that pleases You. I know that I have so many reasons to be thankful. So, let me count my blessings and remember all the good things that have happened to me. Amen

DAY 331

You Will Be Blessed if You Learn How to Share

God has given gifts to each of you from his great variety of spiritual gifts. Manage them well so that God's generosity can flow through you.

1 Peter 4:10 NLT

Jesus said, "It is more blessed to give than to receive." That means that we should be generous with other people–but sometimes we don't feel much like sharing. Instead of sharing the things that we have, we want to keep them all to ourselves. That's when we must remember that God doesn't want selfishness to rule our hearts; He wants us to be generous.

Are you lucky enough to have nice things? If so, God's instructions are clear: you must share your blessings with others. And that's exactly the way it should be. After all, think how generous God has been with you.

TODAY'S PRAYER

Lord, You have been so generous with me; I want to be generous with others. Help me share the things I have, and help me share the love I feel in my heart. Amen

DAY 332

Listen to Your Conscience

I always do my best to have a clear conscience toward God and men.

Acts 24:16 HCSB

Your conscience is a little feeling that will usually tell you what to do and when to do it. Pay attention to that feeling, and trust it.

If you slow down and listen to your conscience, you'll usually stay out of trouble. And if you listen to your conscience, it won't so hard to control your own behavior. Why? Because most of the time, your conscience already knows right from wrong. So don't be in such a hurry to do things. Instead of "jumping right in," listen to your conscience. In the end, you'll be very glad you did.

TODAY'S PRAYER

Dear Lord, in my heart, I know right from wrong. Let me listen to that quiet voice so that I can behave myself and control myself tomorrow and every day after that. Amen

aFTeR you've made a mistake

Then Jesus said, "So I also don't judge you. You may go now, but don't sin again."

John 8:11 ICB

D o you ever make mistakes? Of course you do! Even if you're a very good person, you're bound to make a mistake or two–everybody does.

When you do something you shouldn't have done, here are some things you can do:

1. Apologize to the people you've hurt, and ask for their forgiveness; 2. Fix the things you've messed up or broken; 3. Don't make the same mistake again; 4. Ask God for His forgiveness (which, by the way, He will give to you instantly); 5. Get busy doing something you can be proud of. 6. Don't be too hard on yourself . . . even if you made a mistake, you're still a very, very special person!

TODAY'S PRAYER

Dear Lord, I make mistakes, and when I make them, I'm sorry. Help me be quick to admit my mistakes, and just as quick to ask for forgiveness. Amen

DAY 334

an example for others

We're Christ's representatives. God uses us to persuade men and women to drop their differences and enter into God's work of making things right between them. We're speaking for Christ himself now: Become friends with God; he's already a friend with you.

2 Corinthians 5:20 MSG

What kind of example are you? Are you the kind of boy who shows other people what it means to be kind and forgiving? Hopefully so!

How hard is it to say a kind word? Not very! How hard is it to accept someone's apology? Usually not too hard. So today, be a good example for others to follow. Because God needs people, like you, who are willing to stand up and be counted for Him. And that's exactly the kind of example you should try to be.

TODAY'S PRAYER

Dear Lord, I will praise You by following in the footsteps of Your Son. Help me to be a good example, so that others see Him through me. Amen

DAY 335

THE BEST TIME TO DO HOMEWORK

We can't afford to waste a minute, must not squander these precious daylight hours in frivolity and indulgence, in sleeping around and dissipation, in bickering and grabbing everything in sight. Get out of bed and get dressed! Don't loiter and linger, waiting until the very last minute. Dress yourselves in Christ, and be up and about!

Romans 13:13-14 MSG

Sooner or later, you'll start getting homework, and when that day comes, you'd better be ready because that's when you'll really need lots of self-control! Usually, homework isn't hard to do, but it takes time. And sometimes, we'd rather be doing other things (like playing outside or watching TV). But, when we put off our homework until the last possible minute, we make it hard on ourselves.

Instead of putting off your homework, do it first. Then, you'll have the rest of your time to have fun–and you won't have to worry about all that homework.

TODAY'S PRAYER

Dear Lord, help me do the work I need to do, and help me do it before it needs to be done, not after it needs to be done. Amen

DAY 336

Very Big Ideas About Celebrating Today

To start your day, take a few minutes to talk to your mom or dad about what these two quotations mean.

With each new dawn, life delivers a package to your front door, rings your doorbell, and runs.

Charles Swindoll

Every day we live is a priceless gift of God, loaded with possibilities to learn something new.

Dale Evans Rogers

TODAY'S PRAYER

Dear Lord, I thank You for this wonderful day and for all the blessings You have given me. Now and always, I will be a joyful Christian, quick to smile and slow to frown. Amen

DAY 337

Love Everybody

But love ye your enemies, and do good, and lend, hoping for nothing again; and your reward shall be great, and ye shall be the children of the Highest . . .

Luke 6:35 KJV

I t's easy to love people who have been nice to you, but it's very hard to love people who have treated you badly. Still, Jesus instructs us to treat both our friends and our enemies with kindness and respect.

Are you having problems being nice to someone? Is there someone you know whom you don't like very much? Remember that Jesus not only forgave His enemies, He also loved them . . . and so should you.

A TIP TO START YOUR DAY

How hard is it to love your enemies? You'll never know until you try . . . so try!

TODAY'S PRAYER

Dear Lord, the Bible says I should forgive everybody. So even if my friends are not nice to me, I'll try my best to forgive them and show them what it means to be a Christian. Amen

DAY 338

HAPPINESS AND FORGIVENESS GO TOGETHER

Those who show mercy to others are happy, because God will show mercy to them.

Matthew 5:7 NCV

If you're unwilling to forgive other people, you're building a roadblock between yourself and God. And the less you're willing to forgive, the bigger your roadblock.

If you really want to forgive someone, pray for that person. And then pray for yourself by asking God to help you forgive. Don't expect forgiveness to be easy or quick, but with God as your helper, you can forgive . . . and you will.

TODAY'S PRAYER

Dear Lord, I know that I should forgive people, even when forgiveness is hard. Please give me a forgiving heart, Father, this day and every day. Amen

Heaven Will Be Wonderful!

Be glad and rejoice, because your reward is great in heaven.

Matthew 5:12 HCSB

The Bible makes this important promise: when you give your heart to Jesus, you will live forever with Him in heaven. And Jesus told us that His house has "many mansions" (John 14:1-3).

Even though we don't know everything about heaven, we do know this: heaven will be a wonderful place, a place of joy and wonder, a place where we will be reunited with our loved ones and with God. It's wonderful to think about . . . and a priceless gift from God.

TODAY'S PRAYER

Dear Lord, the Bible promises that heaven is a wonderful place. I thank You, Father, for the gift of eternal life that is mine through Your Son, Jesus. This day and every day, I will keep the promise of heaven in my heart. Amen

TELLING THE TRUTH

Don't ever forget kindness and truth. Wear them like a necklace. Write them on your heart as if on a tablet.

Proverbs 3:3 NCV

When we're dishonest, we make ourselves unhappy and we let other people down. It's easy to see that lies always cause far more problems than they solve. Lies, no matter what size, are never part of God's plan for our lives, so we must tell the truth about everything.

Have you ever said something that wasn't true? When you did, were you sorry for what you had said? Probably (and hopefully) so.

Happiness and honesty always go hand in hand. But it's up to you to make sure that you go hand in hand with them! And besides, when you always tell the truth, you don't have to try and remember what it was that you said!

TODAY'S PRAYER

Dear Lord, the Bible teaches me that it's important to be an honest person. Give me the strength to tell the truth, even when it's hard. Amen

DAY 341

Kindness is a Choice

Love is patient; love is kind.

1 Corinthians 13:4 HCSB

Kindness is a choice. Sometimes, when we feel happy or hopeful, we find it easy to be kind. Other times, when we are sad or tired, we may find it much harder to be kind. But the Bible teaches us to be kind, even when we don't feel like it.

So do everybody (including yourself) a big favor: try to be kind all the time. It's the smart choice and the right thing to do.

A TIP TO START YOUR DAY

Kindness should be part of our lives every day, not just on the days when we feel good. And remember this: small acts of kindness can make a big difference.

TODAY'S PRAYER

Dear Lord, the Bible teaches me to be kind. Help me, Lord, to show kindness to the people I meet, and help me to lend a helping hand whenever I can. Amen

DAY 342

The Time to Talk to God is Now

Then if my people who are called by my name will humble themselves and pray and seek my face and turn from their wicked ways, I will hear from heaven and will forgive their sins and heal their land.

2 Chronicles 7:14 NLT

God promises that He hears your prayers—every one of them! So if you want to say something to God, you can start praying (with your eyes open or shut). Whatever your need, no matter how great or small, pray about it and never lose hope. God is not just near; He is here, and He's ready to talk with you. Now!

A TIP TO START YOUR DAY

You can offer lots of prayers to God all day long . . . and you should!

TODAY'S PRAYER

Dear Lord, thank You for hearing my prayers. I will pray often, and I will follow in the footsteps of Your Son, this day and every day. Amen

DAY 343

TRY TO MEMORIZE THESE VERSES

*For I am persuaded that neither
death nor life, nor angels nor
principalities nor powers,
nor things present nor things to come,
nor height nor depth,
nor any other created thing,
shall be able to separate us
from the love of God
which is in Christ Jesus our Lord.*

Romans 8:38-39 NKJV

*This is an important Bible verse. Practice saying it
several times. And then, talk to your mom or dad
about exactly what the verse means . . .*

A TIP FOR PARENTS
Today, talk to your child about . . .
Christ's everlasting love.

TODAY'S PRAYER
Dear Jesus, I will always thank You for Your
love. Your love never ends. Today, I will
return Your love and I will share it with
the world. Amen

DAY 344

DO WHAT'S RIGHT, AND DO WHAT'S KIND

Let everyone see that you are gentle and kind. The Lord is coming soon.

Philippians 4:5 NCV

Sometimes, it's so much easier to do the wrong thing than it is to do the right thing, especially when we're tired or frustrated. But, doing the wrong thing almost always leads to trouble. And sometimes, it leads to BIG trouble.

When you do the right thing, you don't have to worry about what you did or what you said. But, when you do the wrong thing, you'll be worried that someone will find out. So do the right thing, which, by the way, also happens to be the kind thing. You'll be glad you did, and so will other people!

TODAY'S PRAYER

Dear Lord, I know that You want me to be kind. Help me be a kind person today, tomorrow, and every day after that. Amen

DAY 345

START WITH THE TRUTH

Teach me Your way, O LORD; I will walk in Your truth.

Psalm 86:11 NASB

Sometimes, telling the truth is hard, but even then, it's easier to tell the truth than it is to live with the consequences of telling a lie. You see, telling a lie can be easier in the beginning, but it's always harder in the end! In the end, when people find out that you've been untruthful, they may feel hurt and you will feel embarrassed.

So make this promise to yourself, and keep it: don't let lies rob you of your happiness. Instead, tell the truth from the start. You'll be doing yourself a big favor, and you'll be obeying the Word of God.

TODAY'S PRAYER

Dear Lord, when telling the truth is hard, give me the courage to do what's right. Give me the courage to tell the truth. Amen

DAY 346

Don't Be Afraid To Ask Questions

When doubts filled my mind, your comfort gave me renewed hope and cheer.

Psalm 94:19 NLT

When you're not sure about something, are you willing to ask your parents what you should do? Hopefully, when you have a question, you're not afraid to ask.

If you've got lots of questions, the Bible promises that God–like your parents–has answers, too.

So don't ever be afraid to ask questions. Both your parents and your Heavenly Father want to hear your questions . . . and they want to answer your questions as soon as you ask.

TODAY'S PRAYER

Dear Lord, while I am growing up, I still have so many things to learn. Let me remember that the most important lessons are the ones that I learn every day from my parents and from You. Amen

SELF-CONTROL MATTERS

So prepare your minds for service and have self-control. All your hope should be for the gift of grace that will be yours when Jesus Christ is shown to you.

1 Peter 1:13 NCV

Learning how to control yourself is an important part of growing up. The more you learn about self-control, the better. Self-control will help you at home, at school, and at church. That's why parents and teachers are happy to talk about the rewards of good self-control. And that's why you should be excited about learning how important it is to look before you leap . . . not after!

A TIP TO START YOUR DAY

Sometimes, the best way to control yourself is to slow yourself down. Then, you can think about the things you're about to do before you do them.

TODAY'S PRAYER

Dear Lord, please help me slow myself down and think about things before I do things that I shouldn't do. Amen

DAY 348

VERY BIG IDEAS ABOUT THE WORDS YOU SPEAK

To start your day, take a few minutes to talk to your mom or dad about what these two quotations mean.

Change the heart, and you change the speech.

Warren Wiersbe

If you can't think of something nice to say, keep thinking.

Criswell Freeman

TODAY'S PRAYER

Dear Lord, the Bible teaches me that You hear every word I say. So, I will do my best to say things that are kind, honest, and worthy of Your Son. Amen

DAY 349

WHEN THINGS GO WRONG

I do not consider myself yet to have taken hold of it. But one thing I do: Forgetting what is behind and straining toward what is ahead, I press on toward the goal to win the prize for which God has called me heavenward in Christ Jesus.

Philippians 3:13-14 NIV

When things don't turn out right, it's easy for most of us to give up. Why are we tempted to give up so quickly? Perhaps it's because we're afraid that we might embarrass ourselves if we tried hard but didn't succeed.

When you try hard–and keep trying hard–you can do amazing things . . . but if you quit at the first sign of trouble, you'll miss out. So here's a good rule to follow: when you have something that you want to finish, be brave enough (and wise enough) to finish it . . . you'll feel better about yourself when you do.

TODAY'S PRAYER

Dear Lord, when I am afraid, there are people I can turn to. I thank You, Lord, for the love and support of my family and friends. Help us always to share our concerns with each other, and help us always to take our concerns to You in prayer. Amen

DAY 350

FOLLOWING THE RULES

Here is my final advice: Honor God and obey his commands.

Ecclesiastes 12:13 ICB

Learning how to control yourself helps you become a more obedient person. So the more you learn about self-control, the better.

Learning how to control yourself is a good thing. Self-control helps you at home, at school, and at church. That's why parents and teachers are happy to talk about the rewards of good behavior.

If you want to learn more about self-control, ask your parents. They'll help you figure out better ways to behave yourself. And that's good for everybody . . . especially you!

A TIP TO START YOUR DAY

Be patient, and follow the rules. Even if you don't like some of the rules that you're supposed to follow, follow them anyway.

TODAY'S PRAYER

Dear Lord, help me understand Your rules and obey them, this day and every day. Amen

DAY 351

WHAT is Patience?

Therefore, God's chosen ones, holy and loved, put on heartfelt compassion, kindness, humility, gentleness, and patience.

Colossians 3:12 HCSB

The dictionary defines the word "patience" as "the ability to be calm, tolerant, and understanding." Here's what that means: the word "calm" means being in control of your emotions (not letting your emotions control you). The word "tolerant" means being kind and considerate to people who are different from you. And, the word "understanding" means being able to put yourself in another person's shoes.

If you can be calm, tolerant, and understanding, you will be the kind of person whose good deeds are a blessing to your family and friends. And that's exactly the kind of person that God wants you to be.

TODAY'S PRAYER

Dear Lord, help me become a more patient person. Sometimes I want to rush around and do things too quickly. Slow me down, Lord, and let me become the kind of person You want me to be. Amen

DAY 352

DOING THE RIGHT THING

For the Kingdom of God is not just fancy talk; it is living by God's power.

1 Corinthians 4:20 NLT

Doing the right thing is not always easy, especially when we're tired or frustrated. But, doing the wrong thing almost always leads to trouble. And sometimes, it leads to BIG trouble.

When you do the right thing, you don't have to worry about what you did or what you said. But, if you are dishonest—or if you do something that you know is wrong—you'll be worried that someone will find out. So do the right thing; it may be harder in the beginning, but it's easier in the end.

TODAY'S PRAYER

Dear Lord, sometimes it's easier to misbehave than it is to slow down and think about the best way to behave. But even when doing the right thing is difficult, let me slow down long enough to think about the right thing to say or do. Amen

DAY 353

VERY BIG IDEAS ABOUT HELPING OTHERS

To start your day, take a few minutes to talk to your mom or dad about what these two quotations mean.

Make it a rule, and pray to God to help you to keep it, never, if possible, to lie down at night without being able to say: "I have made one human being at least a little wiser, or a little happier, or at least a little better this day."

Charles Kingsley

Encouraging others means helping people, looking for the best in them, and trying to bring out their positive qualities.

John Maxwell

TODAY'S PRAYER

Dear Lord, Jesus helped other people, and I can, too. Every day, Father, help me be like Jesus as I find ways to help and ways to serve. Amen

Learning the importance of Obedience

You must follow the Lord your God and fear Him. You must keep His commands and listen to His voice; you must worship Him and remain faithful to Him.

Deuteronomy 13:4 HCSB

When you learn to control your actions and your words, you will find it easier to obey your parents, your teachers, and your Father in heaven. Why? Because in order to be an obedient person, you must first learn how to control yourself–otherwise, you won't be able to obey very well, even when you want to.

When you learn the importance of obedience, you'll soon discover that good things happen when you behave yourself. And the sooner you learn to listen and obey, the sooner those good things will start happening.

TODAY'S PRAYER

Dear Lord, I trust You, and I know that Your rules are good for me. I will do my best to obey You, even when it's hard. Amen

GOD CAN HELP YOU BECOME A MORE PATIENT PERSON

Smart people are patient; they will be honored if they ignore insults.

Proverbs 19:11 NCV

A re you a perfectly patient person? If so, feel free to skip the rest of this page. But if you're not, here's something to think about: if you really want to become a more patient person, God is ready and willing to help.

God is always ready to help you become a better person. In fact, the Bible promises that when you sincerely seek God's help, He will give you the things you need. So, if you want to become a more patient person, bow your head and start praying about it. Then, rest assured that with God's help, you can change for the better . . . and you will!

TODAY'S PRAYER

Dear Lord, the Bible tells me that it's better to be patient than impulsive. Help me to slow myself down so I can make better decisions this day and every day. Amen

DAY 356

CHRIST'S Peace

Peace I leave with you. My peace I give to you. I do not give to you as the world gives. Your heart must not be troubled or fearful.

John 14:27 HCSB

The beautiful words of John 14:27 remind us that Jesus offers us peace, not as the world gives, but as He alone gives. We, as believers, can accept His peace or ignore it. When we accept the peace of Jesus Christ into our hearts, our lives are changed forever, and we become more loving, patient Christians.

Christ's peace is offered freely; it has been already been paid for; it is ours for the asking. So let us ask . . . and then share.

A TIP TO START YOUR DAY

Genuine peace is a gift from God. Your job is to accept it.

TODAY'S PRAYER

Dear Lord, You know my heart. Help me to say things, to do things, and to think things that are pleasing to You. Amen

DAY 357

VERY BIG IDEAS ABOUT GOD'S PLANS

To start your day, take a few minutes to talk to your mom or dad about what these two quotations mean.

God is at work; He is in full control; He is in the midst of whatever has happened, is happening, and will happen.

Charles Swindoll

God will never lead you where His strength cannot keep you.

Barbara Johnson

TODAY'S PRAYER

Dear Lord, You have a wonderful plan for this world and a wonderful plan for me. This day and every day, I will do my best to follow Your plan and to obey Your commandments. Amen

DAY 358

Giving to Your Church

In everything I did, I showed you that by this kind of hard work we must help the weak, remembering the words the Lord Jesus himself said: "It is more blessed to give than to receive."

Acts 20:35 NIV

When the offering plate passes by, are you old enough to drop anything in it? If you are, congratulations! But if you're not quite old enough to give money to the church, don't worry—there are still lots of things you can share!

Even when you don't have money to share, you still have much to give to your church. What are some things you can share? Well, you can share your smile, your happiness, your laughter, your energy, your cooperation, your prayers, your obedience, your example, and your love.

So don't worry about giving to the church: even if you don't have lots of money, there are still plenty of ways you can give. And the best time to start giving is NOW!

TODAY'S PRAYER

Dear Lord, help me make Your world a better place. I can't fix all the world's troubles, but I can make things better here at home. Help me remember the importance of sharing the things that I have and the importance of sharing the love that I feel in my heart. Amen

DAY 359

ARE YOU FEELING UPSET OR WORRIED? PRAY ABOUT IT!

I want men everywhere to lift up holy hands in prayer, without anger or disputing.

1 Timothy 2:8 NIV

If you're feeling upset, what should you do? Well, you should talk to your parents and there's something else you can do: you can pray about it.

If there is person you don't like, you should pray for a forgiving heart. If there is something you're worried about, you should ask God to give you comfort. And as you pray more, you'll discover that God is always near and that He's always ready to hear from you. So don't worry about things; pray about them. God is waiting patiently to hear from you . . . and He's ready to listen NOW!

TODAY'S PRAYER

Dear Lord, the Bible says that I should pray often, and that's exactly what I will do now and always. Amen

DAY 360

Very Big Ideas About Being Joyful

To start your day, take a few minutes to talk to your mom or dad about what these two quotations mean.

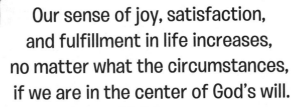

Our sense of joy, satisfaction, and fulfillment in life increases, no matter what the circumstances, if we are in the center of God's will.

Billy Graham

Christ and joy go together.

E. Stanley Jones

TODAY'S PRAYER

Dear Lord, You have given me so many reasons to be happy. I will be a joyful Christian, and I will be thankful for Your gifts. Amen

Safety Matters

The prudent see danger and take refuge, but the simple keep going and suffer from it.

Proverbs 27:12 NIV

Self-control and safety go hand in hand. Why? Because a big part of self-control is looking around and thinking things through before you do something that you might regret later.

Remember the saying "Look before you leap!"? Well if you want to live safely and happily, you should look very carefully before you decide whether or not to leap. After all, it's easy to leap, but once you're in the middle of your jump, it's too late to leap back!

TODAY'S PRAYER

Dear Lord, You protect me; help me to learn how to protect myself. Help me to slow down, to think ahead, and to look before I leap. You are concerned with my safety, Lord. Help me to be concerned with it, too. Amen

DAY 362

When You Don't Understand Something

Immediately the father of the child cried out and said with tears, "Lord, I believe; help my unbelief!"

Mark 9:24 NKJV

Even if you're a very smart boy, you don't know everything! You simply can't understand all the mysteries of God's plans. Nobody can.

Sometimes, people who do nothing wrong get sick; sometimes, innocent people are hurt; sometimes, bad things happen to very good people. These are things that we can't always understand.

But the good news is this: we will have an eternity to have all our questions answered when we get to heaven. And until then, we've simply got to trust God.

TODAY'S PRAYER

Dear Lord, sometimes this world can be a puzzling place. When I am unsure what to do, let me be quick to learn from my parents, and let me be quick to learn from You. Amen

DAY 363

WHAT a FRIEND!

And I am convinced that nothing can ever separate us from his love. Whether we are high above the sky or in the deepest ocean, nothing in all creation will ever be able to separate us from the love of God that is revealed in Christ Jesus our Lord.

Romans 8:38-39 NLT

Jesus loves you very much. And you should love Him, too. When you invite Jesus into your heart, you can be sure that He will prepare a place for you in heaven.

Jesus has promised that heaven will be a wonderful place, a place where you will be protected forever.

Jesus is the best friend this world has ever known. Let Him be your friend, too. His love lasts forever. So, what are you waiting for? Welcome Him into your heart right now.

TODAY'S PRAYER

Dear Lord, You sent Your Son to this world so that I can live with Him forever in heaven. Today and every day, I thank You for Your Son, Jesus, and for His love. Amen

DAY 364

iT's a WonDeRFuL Day To CeLebRaTe!

This is the day the LORD has made. We will rejoice and be glad in it.

Psalm 118:24 NLT

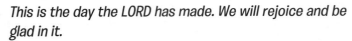

What is the best day to celebrate life? This one! This day and every day should be a time for celebration as we think about all the things God has done for us.

Tomorrow morning, when you wake up, take time to count your blessings. And then, be sure to enjoy yourself. Every day is a gift from your Heavenly Father . . . SO CELEBRATE!

TODAY'S PRAYER

Dear Lord, You have given me so many blessings, too many to count. I will celebrate the life You have given me. And, I will share my joy with my family, with my friends, and with my neighbors, this day and every day. Amen

DAY 365

GOD KNOWS THE RIGHT TIME FOR EVERYTHING

He has made everything beautiful in its time. He has also set eternity in the hearts of men; yet they cannot fathom what God has done from beginning to end.

Ecclesiastes 3:11 NIV

Sometimes, the hardest thing to do is to wait. This is especially true when we're in a hurry and when we want things to happen now, if not sooner! But God's plan does not always happen in the way that we would like or at the time of our own choosing. Still, God always knows best.

Sometimes, even though we may want something very badly, we must still be patient and wait for the right time to get it. And the right time, of course, is determined by God, not by us.

TODAY'S PRAYER

Dear Lord, sometimes I want things to happen in a hurry. But You know what's best for me, and You know when things should happen. Give me the patience to trust Your plans, Lord, not my own. Amen

Mom or Dad Help, Please . . .

WRITE DOWN ONE OF YOUR
FAVORITE VERSES

Now, Draw a Picture about it

YOU PROBABLY LIKE
ALL YOUR VEGGIE FRIENDS.
IS ONE YOUR VERY FAVORITE?

Can you draw and color them?

Mom or Dad Help, Please Help...

WRITE DOWN THE FIRST 4 BOOKS OF THE OLD TESTAMENT

NOW, DRAW A PICTURE ABOUT YOUR FAVORITE STORY
FROM GENESIS, INCLUDE YOUR FAVORITE
VEGGIETALES CHARACTER

Mom or Dad Help, Please Help...

WHAT IS YOUR FAVORITE PLACE TO PLAY OUTDOORS?

CAN YOU DRAW A PICTURE WITH YOU AND YOUR VEGGIE FRIENDS PLAYING THERE?

Smile!
YOUR VEGGIE FRIENDS WOULD LIKE A PICTURE WITH YOU.
ADD YOURSELF INTO THE PICTURE.

DRAW YOURSELF PLAYING WITH
THE VEGGIETALES.

DID YOU KNOW THERE'S GOD MADE ME SPECIAL! FOR GIRLS, TOO?